RWANDA
in Pictures

Tom Streissguth

TF CB

Twenty-First Century Books

Contents

Lerner Publishing Group, Inc., realizes that current information and statistics quickly become out of date. To extend the usefulness of the Visual Geography Series, we developed www.vgsbooks.com, a website offering links to up-to-date information, as well as in-depth material, on a wide variety of subjects. All of the websites listed on www.vgsbooks.com have been carefully selected by researchers at Lerner Publishing Group, Inc. However, Lerner Publishing Group, Inc., is not responsible for the accuracy or suitability of the material on any website other than www.lernerbooks.com. It is recommended that students using the Internet be supervised by a parent or teacher. Links on www.vgsbooks.com will be regularly reviewed and updated as needed.

Website address: www.lernerbooks.com

Twenty-First Century Books
A division of Lerner Publishing Group, Inc.
241 First Avenue North
Minneapolis, MN 55401 U.S.A.

Library of Congress Cataloging-in-Publication Data

Streissguth, Thomas, 1958-
    Rwanda in pictures / by Tom Streissguth.
        p.   cm. — (Visual geography series)
    Includes bibliographical references and index.
    ISBN 978-0-8225-8570-1 (lib. bdg. : alk. paper)
    1. Rwanda—Pictorial works—Juvenile literature. I. Title.
DT450.16.S87 2008
967.571—dc22   2007021324

Manufactured in the United States of America
1 2 3 4 5 6 – PA – 13 12 11 10 09 08

INTRODUCTION

Rwanda, a small, landlocked nation in East Africa, covers a region of mountains, high plateaus, and savanna. Its troubled history includes colonization by Germany and Belgium, civil war, political coups (over-throws of government), and war with neighboring countries. In 1994 the country experienced a genocide (mass murder of a specific racial, political, or cultural group). As many as one million people died at the hands of fellow Rwandans that year.

The roots of many Rwandan troubles lie in a traditional social divide exploited by colonial rulers. In Rwanda a majority group, the Hutu, have lived for centuries alongside a minority group, the Tutsi. Before Rwanda became a European colony, the Hutu made up a large class of farmers and animal herders who didn't own land. The Tutsi owned land and cattle, the marks of wealth and status. Tutsi kings ruled the coun-try, and Tutsi chiefs and subchiefs governed local communities.

The two groups shared a common language and culture. Traditional religion, music, dance, and myth made few distinctions between Hutu

and Tutsi. They lived side by side in rural villages and occasionally intermarried. Through the nineteenth century, Rwanda remained a largely agricultural nation. Nine out of ten Rwandans—Hutu as well as Tutsi—relied on farming to survive. After 1885, when Germany made Rwanda part of the province of Ruanda-Urundi in its colony German East Africa, this pattern did not change.

Nevertheless, social and political tensions developed in the twentieth century. Belgium took control of Ruanda-Urundi in 1916. Afterward, Belgians used the social divide to control the Rwandan administration and economy. They employed Tutsis to govern and manage the colony. Laws forced all Rwandans to carry identity papers, which marked them as Hutu, Tutsi, or Twa (a much smaller indigenous, or native, group). These practices drove Hutus and Tutsis further apart. In the 1950s, the colony began taking steps toward independence. Hutu and Tutsi political parties began competing—sometimes violently—for power.

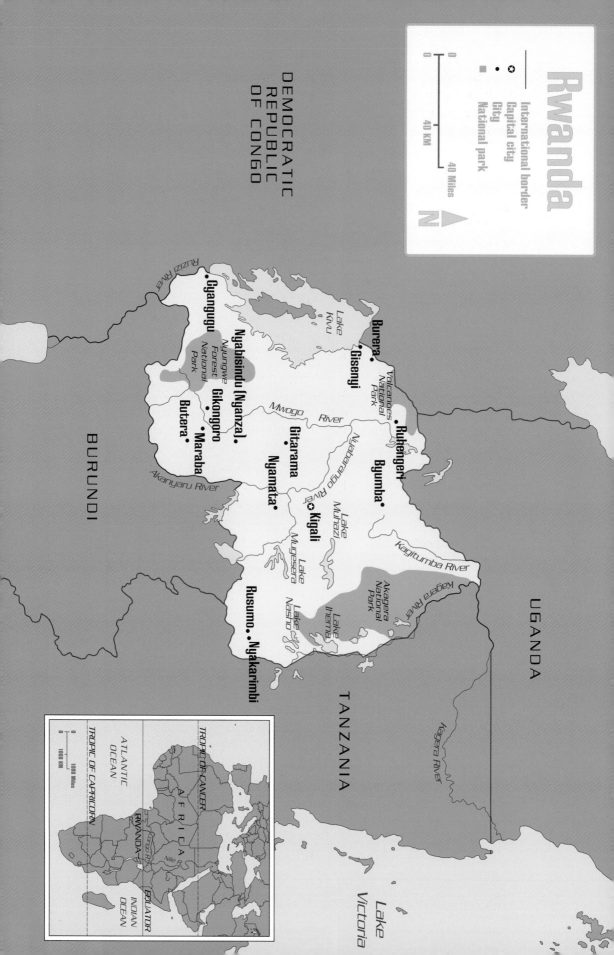

Rwanda gained independence from Belgium in 1962. Afterward, the ongoing power struggle between Hutu and Tutsi leaders set the stage for civil war. A Tutsi militia, or armed group, invaded Rwanda from neighboring Uganda in 1990. The violence quickly spilled over to the civilian population.

In 1994, after the assassination of the Hutu president, rampaging gangs of Hutus went on a murderous spree. They looted, rioted, and killed as many as one million Tutsis and Tutsi supporters. About two million refugees fled the country. The outside world failed to step in and help stop the slaughter.

In the twenty-first century, Rwanda has begun to put these events in the past. It has revived its economy and achieved political stability. Nevertheless, it remains one of the poorest countries in Africa. Its natural resources are limited, and its economy is struggling. Returning refugees find that housing, jobs, and food are scarce. The government relies heavily on foreign development aid and loans. Food donations help a large percentage of Rwandans avoid malnutrition.

Another of Rwanda's most serious challenges is overpopulation. The country is home to about 9.1 million people, giving Rwanda a higher population density than any other mainland African country. Rwandans are mostly farmers, and they have been working the land for centuries. As a result, the country faces a shortage of productive land. The government wants to build a mixed economy that relies on industry and services as well as farming. Achieving this goal, as well as a lasting peace between the country's social groups, are the keys to a better future.

THE LAND

The Republic of Rwanda is a small nation in east central Africa. It shares borders with Uganda on the north, Tanzania on the east, Burundi on the south, and the Democratic Republic of Congo (DRC) on the west. Rwanda's land area is 10,169 square miles (26,338 sq. kilometers), making it slightly smaller than the state of Maryland. The landlocked country has no access to the ocean.

 ## Topography

Most of Rwanda lies at high altitude. The average elevation throughout the country is about 5,200 feet (1,585 meters) above sea level. The topography, or landscape, includes steep hills, densely forested mountains, plateaus (high plains), and savannas (dry grasslands dotted with scrub). Small patches of wilderness survive. But Rwandans use most of the land for crops or animal grazing.

Rwanda has five regions. The Virunga Mountains rise in the northwest, along the border with the DRC and Uganda. This mountain range

includes five volcanoes. One of them, Mount Karisimbi, reaches 14,787 feet (4,507 m)—the country's highest point. The name *Karisimbi* means "white cowrie shell." The name comes from the occasional snow on Karisimbi's peak.

Mount Visoke, the second-highest peak, reaches 12,172 feet (3,710 m). Mount Sabinyo rises 11,930 feet (3,636 m) at the point where the borders of Rwanda, Uganda, and the DRC meet. Rain forest covers the lower slopes of these mountains, while their peaks rise above the timberline.

On the western border of Rwanda is the Albertine Rift Valley region. This region is a branch of the Great Rift Valley running from the Middle East to southern Africa. A rift valley is a deep trough caused by the movement of Earth's crust, or underlying rocky plates. The Albertine Rift Valley runs north and south through a series of lakes in East Africa. It is home to one of the most diverse ecosystems on the continent, including many mammals and birds found nowhere else in the world. Lake Kivu is located in this valley, on Rwanda's western border.

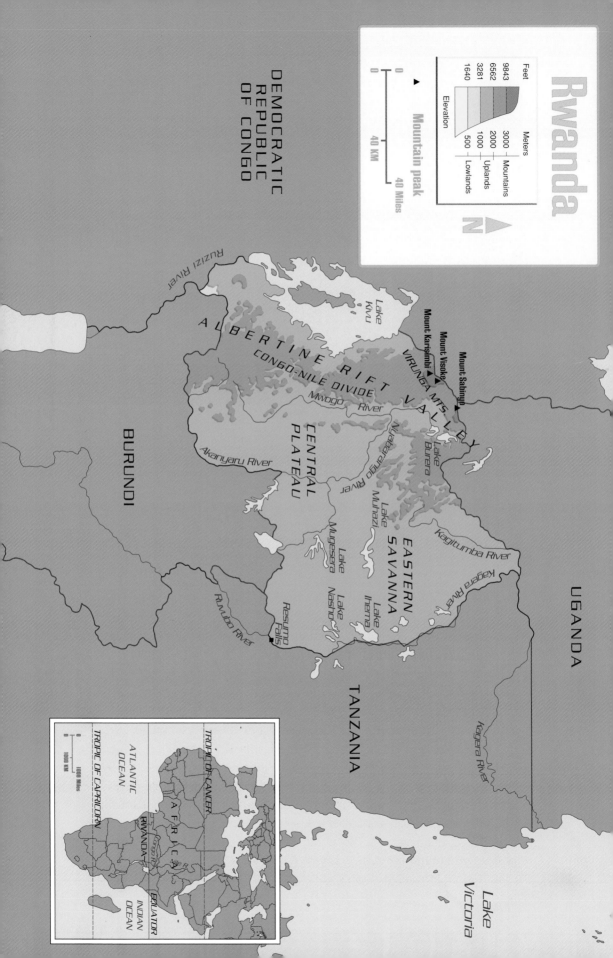

Rwanda

Elevation

Feet	Meters	
9843	3000	Mountains
6562	2000	
3281	1000	Uplands
1640	500	Lowlands

▶ Mountain peak

0 40 KM
0 40 Miles

N

DEMOCRATIC
REPUBLIC
OF CONGO

Ruzizi River

ALBERTINE RIFT VALLEY

Lake Kivu

CONGO-NILE DIVIDE

Mount Karisimbi
Mount Visoke
Mount Sabinyo
VIRUNGA MTS.

Mwogo River

Nyabarongo River

Lake Burera

Lake Ruhondo

CENTRAL PLATEAU

Akanyaru River

Lake Muhazi

EASTERN SAVANNA

Lake Mugesera

Kagitumba River

Kagera River

Lake Nasho

Lake Ihema

BURUNDI

Rumubo River

Resumo Falls

UGANDA

TANZANIA

Kagera River

Lake Victoria

TROPIC OF CANCER

ATLANTIC OCEAN

AFRICA

RWANDA

TROPIC OF CAPRICORN

EQUATOR

INDIAN OCEAN

0 1000 Miles
0 1000 KM

Mist covers the valleys of **Nyungwe Forest National Park** in southwestern Rwanda. The park lies in the Congo-Nile Divide region.

The Congo-Nile Divide region rises east of Lake Kivu in a series of ridges cut by swift streams. The mountains in this region reach about 9,000 feet (2,743 m). Some of the peaks rise over 10,000 feet (3,048 m). They separate the watersheds of (areas drained by) the Congo River to the west and the Nile River to the north. The steep slopes in this region make farming difficult.

East of the Congo-Nile Divide lies a lower region called the Central Plateau. It consists of gently rolling hills. Intensive farming long ago replaced the original forests there. Farming has led to soil erosion, or the washing away of dirt, in some areas. This region has the highest population density in Rwanda and one of the highest densities in Africa.

Rwanda is also known as Pays des Milles Collines, French for "Land of a Thousand Hills."

Farther east the land levels out, with elevations averaging 4,200 feet (1,280 m). This region is called the Eastern Savanna. It includes grassy plains, scrub, wetlands, and lakes. Overgrazing has cleared out brush. Irrigation, or artificial watering, allows intensive cultivation. The wetlands along the eastern border make poor farmland, however, so fewer people live in this area. Akagera National Park covers 1,000 square miles (2,590 sq. km) in the northeast, along Rwanda's border with Tanzania.

Rivers and Lakes

Rwanda lies in a part of Africa commonly called the Great Lakes region. The country straddles two major watersheds. Western Rwanda is part of the Congo River basin. Its rivers flow to the west, eventually entering the Congo River and the Atlantic Ocean. Eastern Rwanda is part of the Nile River basin. Its rivers flow to the east, eventually entering the Nile River and the Mediterranean Sea. Some geographers locate the most distant source of the Nile River in southwestern Rwanda's Nyungwe Forest.

The Mwogo River flows northward along the eastern slopes of the Congo-Nile Divide. The river turns sharply to the southeast and becomes the Nyabarango River and then passes just west of the capital city of Kigali. Several tributaries, or branches, from the mountain slopes join this wide and swift waterway.

The Akanyaru River in the south divides Rwanda and Burundi. This stream flows east and then north, joining the Nyabarango River just south of Kigali.

The Kagera River runs along Rwanda's borders with Burundi and Tanzania, flowing through Lake Nasho and Lake Ihema. The Kagera joins the Kagitumba River at the point where the borders of Rwanda, Uganda, and Tanzania meet. Eventually the river empties into Lake Victoria in Uganda.

Lake Kivu is the largest lake in Rwanda. It covers 1,040 square miles (2,694 sq. km) along Rwanda's western border. Small port towns and resorts dot the shores of Lake Kivu. The Ruzizi River drains the lake to

Volcanic Mount Karisimbi looms over Lake Burera near the town of Ruhengeri.

the south. Lake Muhazi and Lake Mugesera lie in the Central Plateau, northeast and southeast of Kigali.

Climate

Rwanda lies just south of the equator, the halfway point between the North Pole and the South Pole. Its location brings a humid climate with frequent rain. However, its high elevation moderates temperatures. The Rwandan climate is cooler than that of many other equatorial nations.

Rwanda has two dry seasons and two rainy seasons. January and February are dry, followed by a rainy season from March to May. June through September are the driest months of the year. The months of September through December bring frequent, heavy thunderstorms. The highest elevations of the Virunga Mountains sometimes have snow at this time of year.

Trade winds blowing westward from the Indian Ocean bring rain to eastern Africa. As the humid air crosses rising elevations, it cools and forms rain clouds. The clouds then drop rain as they pass over mountain peaks. Southern Rwanda gets about 70 inches (178 centimeters) of rain a year. The southwest and the higher elevations get the most rainfall. The western regions and the Central Plateau receive about 50 inches (127 cm) of rain per year.

In the east, rains are lighter and temperatures are warmer, frequently reaching 90°F (32°C). In Kigali temperatures average 66°F (19°C) from spring through early summer and then turn slightly warmer. (Since Rwanda is south of the equator, its seasons are opposite those of countries north of the equator.) In the western mountains above 9,000 feet (2,743 m), night temperatures can fall below freezing. On the eastern shores of Lake Kivu, the temperature averages 73°F (23°C).

THE EXPLODING LAKE

The calm surface of Lake Kivu hides a serious danger. Carbon dioxide and methane gas saturate the cold water at the bottom of the lake. If the lake were disturbed (for example, by an earthquake or volcanic eruption), the methane could rise to the surface and cause a massive, deadly explosion.

An explosion would release huge amounts of carbon dioxide. In 1986 a carbon dioxide release happened at Lake Nyos, in the western African nation of Cameroon. Almost two thousand people suffocated when the gas pushed aside the area's normal oxygenated air.

More than one million people live along the shores of Lake Kivu. To prevent a catastrophe, engineers plan to install pipes that draw the methane away from the lake. The project is very expensive, however, and work has not yet started.

These greenish **beryl** **crystals** lie between layers of white quartz. Rwanda extracts the mineral for use in the electronic components of cell phones.

Natural Resources

Rwanda has a variety of mineral resources. They include cassiterite (tin ore), wolframite (which contains the useful element tungsten), coltan (an ore refined for electronics manufacturing), some gold, and beryl (a hard mineral that contains the element beryllium, which has many industrial uses). The cost of extracting and refining these minerals is high. The country's most productive mines belong to foreign companies, and Rwanda needs more outside investment to develop new mineral resources.

Rwanda has no oil deposits and must import this fuel. However, researchers have discovered a large field of underground natural gas near Lake Kivu. This gas may help Rwanda meet its own energy needs and earn export income. The country's rivers hold potential for hydroelectric projects, which harness the power of rushing water to produce energy.

Rwanda's fertile soil and abundant water have made it a productive agricultural nation. Despite centuries of farming, some natural forests survive in the mountains of the northwest. The government protects most of this land from logging.

Flora and Fauna

Most of Rwanda's land is cultivated (farmed). About 20 percent of the country remains a natural forest. Higher elevations in the west and northwest remain in their natural state, and the country has set aside preserves there. Some wild stands of bamboo and thorny acacia also remain in Rwanda.

Rwanda's dense population and intensive farming have destroyed natural habitat throughout the country. Though its wildlife is dwindling, elephants, lions, chimpanzees, antelopes, warthogs, and mountain gorillas survive in the Virunga Mountains of the northwest. In the southwest, Nyungwe Forest National Park is home to twelve species of primates, including the vervet monkey, the olive baboon, L'Hoest's monkey, and the Ruwenzori colobus monkey. Lush flora, including more than one hundred native orchid species, cover the park.

In the savanna of eastern Rwanda, a few remote areas are still rich in mammal and bird species. Akagera National Park protects small populations of hippopotamuses, bushbucks, warthogs, buffalo, giraffes, elands, leopards, lions, hyenas, topis, and zebras. The lakes and marshes of the region provide a natural refuge for many species of water-birds. Egrets, storks, ibises, pelicans, and herons thrive there.

Environmental Issues

The natural environment is under strain in modern Rwanda. The growth of cities has caused both air and water pollution. The government enforces few pollution controls for vehicles, which clog the city streets and cloud the air with exhaust.

The refugee crisis of the 1990s also damaged Rwanda's natural environment. Desperate people streamed out of the cities and took shelter in wilderness areas near the border. To survive, they cut down trees for firewood and foraged plants for food. In some areas, they left the land completely bare.

Most farming families in this densely populated country survive from the produce of very small fields. In search of new land to cultivate, many are moving into the forests, clearing trees, and sowing rows of plantains (a kind of banana), cassava (a starchy root crop), and other food plants. Some farmers are moving to steep hillsides at higher elevations. Farming these areas damages the land even more, because heavy rains easily wash away topsoil that is not anchored by natural vegetation. The soil ends up as sediment that clogs waterways.

Rwanda is steadily losing natural habitat. When farmers divert rivers to irrigate their crops, the rivers dry up and animals must move in search of food and water. This is a common problem in eastern Rwanda, where many wetlands are disappearing.

A **L'Hoest's monkey** keeps watch from the safety of a tree. The monkeys spend most of their time on the ground, using trees to escape predators.

Wildlife is also dwindling due to poaching (illegal hunting) in Rwanda's national forests and other wilderness areas. Hunters trap or shoot elephants, antelopes, and primates and sell the carcasses secretly. Many people poach animals simply to feed their families. The government has passed hunting regulations but cannot afford to hire enough game officers to enforce the laws.

Cities

KIGALI (population of the city and province: 789,330) is the capital and largest city of Rwanda. Lying in the center of the country, it covers a series of hills and valleys. The main streets and markets are in the valleys. The residential areas spread across the hillsides. The city is sprawling in all directions as newcomers arrive from the countryside.

Kigali was founded in 1907. At that time, Rwanda was a part of Ruanda-Urundi, a province of the colony of German East Africa. Kigali's location was convenient for traders and missionaries, or religious teachers, who could easily travel from there to all other parts of the province.

In 1962, when Rwanda gained independence, Kigali became the national capital. Butare was initially the leading contender, but Kigali

Pedestrians go about their business on a street in Kigali.

won because of its more central location. Kigali has been the economic, cultural, and transport hub of Rwanda ever since. The official home and offices of the Rwandan president, as well as all government ministries, or departments, are in Kigali. This city is also the seat of the Rwandan parliament, or legislature.

Beginning April 7, 1994, Kigali became the scene of tragic events. Strife between Hutus and Tutsis exploded into genocide. Kigali's streets filled with rampaging mobs armed with guns and machetes. The fighting continued for months and destroyed thousands of homes, shops, and small factories. It finally ended when the Rwandan Patriotic Front (RPF), a Tutsi militia, took control of Kigali in July 1994. Although heavily damaged, the city has gradually recovered.

Main roads from neighboring Uganda, Tanzania, and Burundi join in Kigali. The city is also home to Kigali International Airport, which provides Rwanda's only air routes to foreign countries. City engineers are drawing up plans for a new, larger airport in Nyamata, about 25 miles (40 km) away.

RUHENGERI (province population: 891,498), in the northwest, is the main departure point for visitors to Volcanoes National Park. Mount Karisimbi, the highest mountain in Rwanda, rises just outside the city.

GITARAMA (province population: 856,488) is a transportation hub and market center. It is located about 50 miles (85 km) west of Kigali.

BUTARE (also called Huye, city and province population 725,914) in the southwest was the cultural and political center before Rwanda gained independence. The National University of Rwanda and the National Museum of Rwanda are both in Butare. A small town near Butare called Nyabisindu is the former Nyanza, once the seat of Rwanda's monarchs. Nyabisindu's large replica of the traditional royal palace attracts visitors.

CYANGUGU (province population: 607,495) is a resort area on the southern shore of Lake Kivu. It lies near a main border crossing into the DRC and Burundi.

Visit www.vgsbooks.com for links to websites with additional information about Rwanda, including travel guidelines and advisories. Learn about efforts to preserve Rwanda's natural resources and to protect endangered species.

HISTORY AND GOVERNMENT

Archaeologists have found the oldest fossils of human ancestors in the Great Rift Valley. Part of this valley runs along the western border of Rwanda, as the Albertine Rift Valley. Scientists believe humans spread out from this locale to settle Asia, Europe, and eventually the rest of the globe.

About five thousand years ago, the climate of the Albertine Rift Valley and the rest of the Great Lakes region changed. Rainfall decreased, and the weather became warmer. The rain forests of East Africa changed to savanna. Water levels in the lakes and rivers fell, and many wetlands dried up completely.

At the same time, wild game may have grown scarce. To survive, humans had to change their way of life. Once nomadic (wandering) hunters, fishers, and food gatherers, people settled down and began farming. They cleared land and planted crops. They tamed wild animals, such as cattle, and began raising them for meat and milk.

By about A.D. 1000, Rwanda was the scene of dense human settle-

ment. The inhabitants cut trees for firewood and cleared hilltops to create more cropland. Farmers grew yams and grains such as sorghum and millet. In well-watered, low-lying areas, some farmers also raised bananas. This crop came to East Africa aboard trading ships from Southeast Asia. People built large villages along the shores of Lake Kivu.

Early Rwanda had many centers of pottery production. In some places, the people made iron goods by heating iron-bearing rock in open-pit fires. Blacksmiths fashioned a variety of tools, ceremonial items, and weapons from iron.

The Society Divides

Historians believe the Twa people have been living in Rwanda for more than five hundred years. They are related to other people of small stature who live in the Congo River basin to the west. The Twa traditionally lived as hunter-gatherers and potters in the remote northern rain forests of Rwanda. They have always been a very small minority group, living apart from the Tutsi and Hutu.

The divide between the Tutsi and Hutu goes back several hundred years, well before any written history in Rwanda. Many historians believe that Tutsi cattle herders first entered Rwanda from the Nile River basin to the north and settled in the region of Lake Muhazi. They moved from place to place in search of water and good pasture for their cows, which provided meat, milk, and wealth. At about the same time, the Hutu migrated into Rwanda from the Congo River basin to the west. The Hutu were farmers and food gatherers. They saw their *bahinza* (kings) as semidivine rulers who could bring rain and protect crops.

The Tutsi made up a smaller, wealthier class of village chiefs, landowners, and kings. They controlled cattle herds, historically the main source of wealth in Rwanda. The Hutu were farmers who worked the Tutsis' land and owned little property of their own. They formed a poorer majority—the working class of traditional Rwandan society.

Ubuhake and Uburetwa

The division between Tutsi and Hutu followed social and economic systems known as ubuhake (for ownership of cattle) and uburetwa (for distribution of land). The cattle-owning and landowning Tutsi made up the aristocracy, while the Hutu served as farmers and herders. A Tutsi *mwami* (king) ruled over this system.

The mwami presided at a *biru*, or council of Tutsi chiefs. They advised him on important matters and on his responsibilities. (For example, the mwami was expected to appease the spirits in times of drought or other natural disaster.) The biru were expert in court ritual and in the proper duties and roles of the chiefs. They also chose the king's successor from an aristocratic clan (extended family).

A museum occupies the site of the **King's Palace,** the traditional dwelling of the mwami (Tutsi king). This re-creation of the Palace is in Nyanza.

The chiefs and subchiefs ruled *umosozi*, small domains centered on the fertile hilltops. Each domain had a chief of land and a chief of cattle, who were responsible for collecting taxes and resolving disputes.

The frontiers of Rwanda were sites of frequent conflict. The chiefs of these regions were responsible for defending their domains and raiding Rwanda's neighbors. Rwanda and Burundi competed for land and control of cattle and trade. The mwami also had to deal with Hutu people of the mountainous northwest. These Hutu, as well as the Twa hunter-gatherers in the same region, lived independently and never fully submitted to mwami control.

Rwandan Kingdoms

The Great Lakes region was a complex patchwork of communities. Each community controlled land and resources in a small area—a few hilltops, the headwaters of a river, or the shores of a lake. Through alliances and warfare, a few dynasties (ruling families) emerged and conquered larger domains. Central governments remained weak, however. Power rested with chiefs, who led the many semi-independent communities and clans.

The Abanyiginya emerged as the royal clan of Rwanda some time before the sixteenth century. These rulers frequently battled with the Gisaka dynasty, which held the Kagera River valley to the east. In the

1500s, a Gisaka enemy killed Ruganzu Bwimba, one of the first Abanyiginya kings. Bwimba's son, Cyrima Rugwe, struck back with frequent raids and extended his authority into eastern Rwanda. Later, the Banyoro people from the north invaded and destroyed this domain. The invasion forced Mwami Mibambwe Mutabazi I to flee beyond Lake Kivu.

In the early seventeenth century, Mwami Ruganzu Ndori emerged to revive the Rwandan kingdom. His successors expanded the domain west to Lake Kivu and east to the Gisaka lands. The monarchy consolidated its territory to the modern borders of Rwanda and defeated its rival Burundi kings in battle.

Yuhi IV Gahindiro ruled Rwanda in the 1830s. He expanded the monarchy's control northward. Mwami Kigeri Rwabugiri, who reigned from 1860 to 1895, led invasions north of the Virunga Mountains into southern Uganda. Rwabugiri established a center of power in western Rwanda.

At this time, Rwanda was one of the largest and most powerful kingdoms in East Africa. Rwandan farmers migrated to remote corners of the realm to establish new farms and homesteads. The Tutsi *bami* (kings; plural of *mwami*) grew wealthy from trade and could summon large armies on short notice. These forces posed a serious and constant threat to smaller neighboring kingdoms in what became Uganda, Burundi, and Tanzania.

European Conquest

In the mid-nineteenth century, European exploration of East Africa began. British explorers John Speke and Richard Burton voyaged in the

Richard Burton

Congo River basin and the Great Lakes region in 1857 and 1858. Beginning in the 1880s, German explorers worked their way inland from the Indian Ocean coast. But no European had yet reached Rwanda.

Europeans sought colonies in Africa to exploit the continent's land and natural resources. They believed African territories might hold deposits of valuable minerals. They also hoped Africans would provide a large pool of cheap labor for European companies.

At the Conference of Berlin in 1885, representatives from many European nations decided that Rwanda would become part of Ruanda-Urundi. Ruanda-Urundi included the kingdoms of Rwanda and Burundi. By the General Act of the Berlin Conference, Rwanda belonged to Germany—even though no Europeans had yet set foot there.

The Kagera River tumbles through a valley and over **Rusumo Falls.**

In 1894 the German explorer Gustav Adolf von Goetzen became the first European to reach Rwanda. He arrived at the kingdom's eastern frontier with two companions. The party made its way west to the shores of Lake Kivu and the Virunga Mountains. It found a densely populated land, governed by a complex political system headed by a king and greatly feared by its neighbors.

Europeans also came to Rwanda as Christian missionaries. The German Catholic Church set up missions to teach and preach throughout German East Africa. These became important way stations for trade, traffic, and communication among explorers and merchants. Germans gave Africans who converted to Christianity positions of responsibility in the colony.

Rwanda occupied a crossroads connecting the Congo River basin, Lake Victoria, and the East African coast. Belgium, which held the area that would become the Democratic Republic of Congo (DRC), and Great Britain contested possession of Rwanda. But Germany continued to send explorers, missionaries, and settlers. In 1907 a German envoy,

Richard Kandt, built an outpost at Kigali. A small market town grew around the post, which became the center of the colonial government.

Under German control, the ubuhake and uburetwa systems continued in Ruanda-Urundi. The Germans governed the colony through its mwami. Germany also provided weapons and soldiers to help the mwami suppress the defiant Hutus of the northwest. In 1912 an expeditionary force ventured into northern Rwanda to squash a Hutu rebellion and put its leader to death.

In the meantime, missionaries were building schools and churches and converting Rwandans to Christianity. Hutus with some European education managed to make a living outside the ubuhake and uburetwa systems that kept most Hutus in service to Tutsis. The German governor appointed Hutus to help administer the colony. Eventually the governor began collecting from each household a head tax that depended on the number of individuals living there. These actions gave the colonists more direct authority over Rwandans and further weakened Tutsi control over the Hutu.

Rwanda had fertile land and a temperate climate. The colony began producing coffee and tea for export. European companies came to look for minerals. They found only small deposits, so Rwanda remained a largely agricultural colony.

Belgian Control

World War I (1914–1918) broke out in Europe in 1914. Germany invaded Belgium and France and also fought the British. In East Africa, German forces were far weaker than those of Belgium. In 1916 Germany withdrew most of its troops from Ruanda-Urundi, and Belgian forces marched in. Belgium supported the economic control of Rwanda by Tutsi cattle herders and chiefs but strictly limited the mwami's authority.

At the end of World War I in 1918, Belgium still occupied Ruanda-Urundi. At the Paris Peace Conference in 1919, the victorious nations (the Allies) officially recognized Belgian control. The countries established the League of Nations at the conference. The league authorized Belgian administration of the colony.

In 1925 Belgium joined Ruanda-Urundi to the Belgian Congo (modern DRC), making it a province of its western neighbor. A governor-general ruled the colony of Rwanda from the city of Usumbura (present-day Bujumbura, the capital of modern Burundi).

Like the Germans, the Belgians ruled through the Tutsi, built missions and schools, and produced coffee as a cash crop. Belgium passed new laws ending the offices of land chief, cattle chief, and military chief. In each district of the colony, the Belgians replaced the traditional leaders with European governors. But Belgium also supported the Tutsi chiefs and did nothing to ease the tensions brewing between Hutus and Tutsis.

The Belgians deposed (removed) Mwami Yuhi Musinga in 1931. The Belgian colonial governor bypassed the biru and selected Charles Mutara III Rudahigwa (commonly called Mutara III) as the new mwami. The Belgian authorities also created an artificial social division, classifying any person owning ten or more cattle as Tutsi.

In 1939 war broke out again in Europe. During World War II (1939–1945), Rwanda took its first steps toward representative government. A 1943 law established elected advisory councils. These councils were supposed to advise the mwami in matters of trade, business, and taxation.

Hutu and Tutsi Conflict

As World War II was ending in 1945, the United Nations (UN) replaced the League of Nations. As part of its job of settling international disputes, the UN tried to resolve conflicts over European colonies in Africa. In 1946 the UN confirmed Belgian control of Ruanda-Urundi. By UN

Mwami Mutara III *(left)* meets with Armand Denis, a Belgian wildlife photographer and filmmaker, in 1936.

mandate, Belgium brought Rwandans into the government. Rwanda also began to build democratic political institutions.

In July 1952, the colonial authorities passed a decree creating elected councils in local towns and provinces. But the Tutsi chiefs remained in control by reserving the right to nominate candidates. At the same time, the ubuhake system began to change. The Tutsi kept their land ownership, but the colony began to redistribute cattle to Hutu farmers.

As Rwanda moved toward self-government, the strains between Hutu and Tutsi increased. Seeking more control over the country, the Tutsi demanded independence. The Hutu, however, wanted Belgian control to continue. They believed that European governors would help the Hutu gain some political and economic equality with the Tutsi.

In 1959 Mwami Mutara III was assassinated. This event sparked political conflict. The Tutsi biru named Mutara's younger brother, Kigeli V Ndahindurwa, as the new mwami. Tutsi leaders formed the Rwanda National Union Party (UNAR) to demand total independence. UNAR favored a new constitution that would preserve the Rwandan monarchy.

Meanwhile, the Hutu formed their own political parties, including Aprosoma in 1957 and Parmehutu in 1959. With the support of the Belgian authorities, Parmehutu sought land ownership reform, access to education for all, and an end to Tutsi domination.

When the Hutu parties led demonstrations in the capital, however, the colonial governor banned political meetings and rallies. Tensions increased until November 1, 1959, when UNAR members attacked a

A soldier of the army of the Belgian Congo guards Hutu rioters arrested in November 1959.

Rwandan men vote for new municipal leaders in the city of Usumbura in 1960. When Belgium split its colony into two countries, Rwanda and Burundi, Usumbura was renamed Bujumbura and became the capital of Burundi.

Parmehutu member, Dominique Mbonyumutwa, in the streets. Nationwide violence erupted. Hutu mobs marched through villages and towns and killed Tutsi chiefs. Thousands of Tutsis fled the country to refugee camps in the neighboring colony of Belgian Congo, as well as to Uganda and Tanzania. To calm the situation, Belgium ordered troops into Rwanda.

Independence

Seeking to stop the violence and answer the calls for political independence, the Belgian administration held elections in the summer of 1960. These elections established the new office of *bourgmestre*. Bourgmestres were local governors who administered 229 new communes (counties). Residents of each commune elected members of a local council, whose authority replaced that of the local Tutsi chief. This system gave more power to the Hutu majority. Rwandans elected 210 Hutus and only 19 Tutsis to the office of bourgmestre. In protest, the Tutsi mwami went into exile. He moved to the former Belgian Congo, which had gained its independence from Belgium that year.

In October 1960, Rwandans set up a new provisional (temporary) government. Grégoire Kayibanda, the leader of Parmehutu, served as the head of this government. In January 1961, Mbonyumutwa led a revolt that overthrew the Tutsi monarchy. Elections for a new legislature took place in September 1961. Parmehutu won nearly 80 percent

President **Juvénal Habyarimana** speaks before the Rwandan parliament in 1993.

of the vote. A legislative assembly began meeting in October 1961. Rwanda then held a national referendum (vote), which favored full independence.

In January 1962, Belgium gave authority to the provisional government. The government then proclaimed the founding of the Republic of Rwanda. The local council members and mayors made Kayibanda the new Rwandan president. The UN ended Belgian control on June 27, 1962. On July 1, 1962, Rwanda won its complete independence.

Kayibanda remained president until 1973, when Juvénal Habyarimana overthrew him. Under Habyarimana the country grew increasingly divided and violent. Tutsis continued to flee Rwanda into Uganda and Burundi.

In 1986 the Tutsi leader Paul Kagame formed a militia called the Rwandan Patriotic Front (RPF) in Uganda. In 1990 the RPF invaded Rwanda. This sparked a civil war. To counter the invasion, Rwandan Hutu officials trained armed bands of Hutu civilians, known collectively as Interahamwe. These bands fought the RPF and carried out violent reprisals against Tutsi civilians.

In August 1993, the Rwandan government and the RPF leaders met in Tanzania. There they signed an agreement known as the Arusha Accords. This treaty divided power among the RPF and five political parties. It limited the authority of President Habyarimana. Hutu leaders lost their control of the Rwandan army. The accords also required 40 percent of the army to be made up of RPF members.

Genocide

The Arusha Accords did not settle Rwanda's ethnic and political conflicts. Fighting continued even after a UN peacekeeping force called the United Nations Assistance Mission for Rwanda (UNAMIR) arrived. UNAMIR was too small to keep the peace. Although its commanders reported the growing violence to the UN, the organization failed to send reinforcements.

The RPF attacked government outposts, while Hutu militia members continued attacking Tutsi civilians and Hutus supporting the Arusha Accords. On April 6, 1994, President Habyarimana and Cyprien Ntaryamira, the president of Burundi, died when a surface-to-air missile destroyed their plane over the Kigali airport. The government appointed Theodore Sindikubwabo, who had served as the minister of health in Habyarimana's administration, to replace him.

No one knew who had shot down Habyarimana's plane. Nonetheless, his death sparked a series of mass reprisals. Over several months, the Interahamwe and the Rwandan army carried out a genocide of the Tutsi population. Government ministers and radio stations

Soldiers of the Rwandan Patriotic Front travel toward Kigali in 1994. They will join rebels already fighting for control of the city.

controlled by the government issued instructions and urged their Hutu followers to murder Tutsis and any Hutus who interfered. According to most sources, between eight hundred thousand and one million people—most of them Tutsi—died in the massacres.

In the meantime, the RPF gradually seized control of Rwanda. On July 4, 1994, the rebels captured Kigali, forcing Sindikubwabo to flee the country. Kagame and the RPF established a new Government of National Unity. Fearing a wave of revenge killings, about two million Hutus fled Rwanda. Most crossed the western border into the DRC (then called Zaire).

The Hutu and Tutsi refugees filled massive camps of temporary shelters. The Rwandan army invaded eastern Zaire to fight Hutu militias there. The fighting touched off a rebellion in Zaire against its president. It also prompted Uganda to invade Zaire. Refugees escaping the fighting flooded towns and camps throughout eastern Africa.

Genocide and war threw Rwandan society into chaos. The economy ground to a stop. Kigali was largely in ruins, while villages

Displaced Rwandan Hutus gather at the edge of Kimbumba refugee camp in 1995. The camp, established near Goma in the DRC, was home to more than two hundred thousand refugees.

Children in Butare listen to a **transistor radio.**

RADIO PLAYS A ROLE

Many Rwandans are suspicious of government-controlled radio stations—for good reason. Radio played a key role in the 1994 genocide. One station, Radio Télévision Libre des Milles Collines (RTLM or, Free Radio Television of a Thousand Hills), broadcast urgent appeals to Hutu gangs to attack their Tutsi neighbors. The broadcasts continued for weeks in the spring of 1994. After the genocide, three officers of the station stood trial for war crimes. Since then the government has strictly limited political discussions on radio stations. Candidates for office get only a few hours to express their views and are not supposed to identify themselves as Hutu or Tutsi.

throughout Rwanda became ghost towns and farmsteads emptied of livestock and workers. Meanwhile, the governments of Rwanda and Uganda threatened war. Each accused the other of helping antigovernment rebellions.

War in the DRC

In late 1994, a Hutu leader of the RPF named Pasteur Bizimungu became the new president of Rwanda. Kagame became the vice president. Bizimungu and Kagame disagreed bitterly over government policy. They also had to deal with conflict on Rwanda's western border.

The Hutu refugees, many of them members of the Interahamwe, had set up large camps in eastern Zaire. Armed by their allies in Uganda, the Hutus threatened to return to Rwanda and overthrow the new regime. Rwandans in Zaire also supported a rebel force seeking to overthrow the long-standing government of Mobutu Sese Seko, Zaire's president.

In 1996 the conflict escalated into a war in Zaire, later called the First Congo War (1996–1997). Thousands of Rwandans joined in the drive to overthrow the government of Zaire, which succeeded in 1997. Laurent Kabila, the Zairean rebel leader, renamed his country the Democratic Republic of Congo. In response to public criticism for involving a foreign nation in his government, Kabila threw his Rwandan advisers out of Kinshasa, the DRC's capital city. The Rwandan advisers fled to eastern DRC, where they began supporting a rebellion against Kabila's government brewing in the city of Goma. At the same time, the government of Rwanda began claiming DRC land west of Lake Kivu.

In the fall of 1998, war broke out again—the Second Congo War (1998–2003)—when the anti-Kabila rebellion flared in eastern DRC. This time several African nations, including Rwanda, Burundi, and Uganda, entered the fray. The warring nations declared a cease-fire in the summer of 1999. Rwanda signed the Lusaka Agreement in July, but fighting between Rwandan and Ugandan forces continued. The DRC accused Rwanda and Uganda of exploiting minerals, diamonds, and other resources in eastern DRC.

Recent Events

In March 2000, Bizimungu resigned and Kagame became the new president of Rwanda. His government signed another peace agreement with the DRC in 2002. Rwanda began withdrawing its troops later in the year. Armed Hutu groups remained in the DRC, vowing to attack and overthrow the Tutsi-dominated Rwandan government.

In July 2007, Rwanda became the one hundredth country in the world to pass a law banning capital punishment. The new law changed the sentences of about six hundred people awaiting execution in Rwandan prisons.

Bizimungu criticized Kagame's administration and formed the Party for Democracy and Renewal (PDR). The government immediately banned this leading opposition party and arrested Bizimungu in 2002.

In 2003 Rwanda signed a new agreement with Uganda and the United Nations High Commissioner for Refugees (UNHCR). In the same year, Rwanda wrote a new constitution.

In 2004 Bizimungu stood trial on charges of embezzling (stealing) government money, forming an illegal militia, and inciting violence against the state. He was found guilty and sentenced to fifteen years in prison. Kagame pardoned Bizimungu in 2007.

Clothes belonging to victims of the Rwandan genocide hang in a memorial site near Gikongoro. Memorials like this offer Rwandans, many of whom were not able to hold traditional funerals for loved ones, a place to grieve.

Rwanda has largely recovered from the 1994 genocide. Memorial sites throughout the country and an annual day of mourning help Rwandans remember the tragedy and grieve for lost friends and family. However, refugees in neighboring countries still fear reprisals if they return. The plight of refugees and the continuing threat of war in eastern DRC are serious issues that will affect Rwanda's future.

Visit www.vgsbooks.com for links to websites with additional information about Rwanda's efforts to heal after years of violence. Learn the names of the country's leaders and follow recent decisions of Rwanda's parliament.

◉ Government

The constitution of 2003 divided Rwanda into five large provinces (Northern, Eastern, Southern, Western, and Kigali City) and thirty districts. A governor oversees each province, and an elected mayor and district council serve each district.

TRYING GENOCIDE

In November 1994, the UN established the International Criminal Tribunal for Rwanda (ICTR). This court, which meets in Tanzania, tries people accused of crimes during the Rwandan genocide of 1994. The court has a big job on its hands. Hundreds of government officials and private citizens participated in the genocide by planning it, distributing weapons, or urging others to murder. By August 2006, the ICTR had tried twenty-eight accused people, which resulted in twenty-five convictions. Trials involving twenty-seven more accused were in progress, and fourteen additional accused were awaiting trial. Some of the accused are not yet in custody. They have fled Rwanda and are either hiding or dead. The ICTR will be holding trials for many years to come.

Survivors of the 1994 genocide learn about their role as judges in the traditional justice system, which is called Gacaca. These community courts handle the thousands of people accused of less serious crimes during the months of genocidal violence.

Rwanda has a bicameral (two-chamber) parliament. The Chamber of Deputies has eighty members. Direct elections select fifty-three of these members. Provincial councils elect twenty-four women members, the National Youth Council elects two members, and the Federation of Associations of the Disabled elects one. Deputies serve five-year terms.

The Senate has twenty-six members. Local government councils elect twelve of the senators. The president appoints eight senators, a government department called the Political Parties Forum chooses four, and academic institutions elect two. Senators serve eight-year terms.

The president is the head of state. A nationwide popular vote elects the president to a term of seven years. The president can serve only two terms. The president appoints a Cabinet of Ministers to lead the various government departments.

Rwanda has kept the justice system Germany and Belgium built. Courts of first instance hear minor criminal and civil cases. Rwanda's provincial courts hear major cases. Appeals courts reconsider lower court decisions. A court of cassation allows those in a civil or criminal case to bring a final appeal. A Supreme Court of six justices decides important law and policy matters, and a court of accounts deals with public finances. A court of state security tries charges of treason and national security cases.

In 2001 Rwanda established a new system of Gacaca courts to try genocide cases. The Gacaca court harks back to the Rwandan tradition of settling disputes in village assemblies, where everyone involved had a chance to speak.

THE PEOPLE

Rwanda's population is about 9.1 million. It has the highest population density in mainland Africa. An average of 895 people live in every square mile (339 per sq. km) of Rwanda. Experts estimate that the nation's population will grow 28 percent by 2025 to 13.8 million people.

Rwanda is a rural country, with few large towns. About 80 percent of its people live in the country, on hills that support small family farms and pasture. The river valleys and lowlands have fewer people. These areas have a hotter, more humid climate and also are prone to flooding. Northwestern Rwanda has a higher population density than the lake district of the southeast.

Conflict in and around Rwanda since the 1990s has created a large population of Rwandan refugees. Both Hutu and Tutsi families have taken shelter in neighboring countries, including the Democratic Republic of Congo (DRC), Uganda, and Tanzania. Although some have returned, in 2007 about one hundred thousand Rwandans remained in

refugee camps. The camps lack clean water, adequate food supplies, sanitation, electricity, and other basic features.

The Twa, in the meantime, have lost much of the forest they once depended on to survive. Clearing for pasture has largely destroyed the Nyungwe Forest and other forests. Conservation projects in Rwanda's national parks removed Twa households and villages by force. No longer able to live from hunting and gathering, the Twa have largely become laborers and artisans. Many struggle to survive at the bottom of Rwanda's social ladder.

Ethnic Groups

The Rwandan people have historically belonged to three main ethnic groups: Hutu, Tutsi, and Twa. In the twenty-first century, about 90 percent of Rwandans identify themselves as Hutu, 9 percent as Tutsi, and 1 percent as Twa.

Historians have long debated the nature of these divisions. Some

A **Tutsi family** *(left)* stands outside their mud-brick house. Four **Hutu boys** *(above)* smile for a photographer visiting the refugee camp where they live.

historians believe that the Hutu (as well as the Twa) were smaller, darker-skinned people who came from the rain forests and lowlands west of Rwanda. The same historians believe the Tutsi were taller, slenderer, lighter-skinned people who came from northeastern Africa, in the valley of the upper Nile River and its tributaries.

Other historians maintain that *Hutu* and *Tutsi* are simply names for different social classes. These historians say Hutus and Tutsis belong to a single ethnic group that has inhabited Rwanda since the time of the earliest mwami.

The Twa people were traditionally hunters and gatherers who lived in small, remote communities in Rwanda's highlands. In Rwandan society, they have always been outsiders. Under colonial rule, some Twa moved to towns and missions to work as laborers and artisans. They also worked as guardians, entertainers, and servants in the royal courts.

Whatever the true origins of the Hutu, Tutsi, and Twa, European colonists found these divisions useful in ruling Rwanda. In the European view, the Hutu made up the peasantry of Rwanda, while the Tutsi were landowners who dominated the country's government. European manipulation of Rwanda's ethnic groups contributed to violent conflict between Hutus and Tutsis, which led to the genocide of 1994. This conflict occurred even though Hutu and Tutsi have largely blended into a single nationality. Hutus and Tutsis speak the same language and share a common culture, cuisine, and family organization.

Marriage and Family

The basic unit of Rwandan society is the *inzu* (extended family). Inzu members live within a *rugo*, or homestead, a fenced compound that includes homes and gardens. The head of the inzu—usually the eldest male—makes important decisions, helps settle arguments, and decides punishments.

A Rwandan inzu usually includes grandparents, aunts, uncles, and sometimes cousins. Polygyny (having more than one wife) was once common among the Hutu and Tutsi but has largely died out. Sons stay under their father's authority until his death. The family then divides its property evenly among the sons.

Several inzus may consider themselves related through a common male ancestor. Such a kinship group is called an *umuryango*. The male members of the umuryango elect a leader called an *umukungu*.

The largest social group in Rwanda is the *ubwoko* (clan). Rwandans belong to thirteen clans throughout the country. The Abanyiginya clan was the royal clan from which the mwami were selected. Although Rwanda has abolished its monarchy, its clans have survived. Every individual in the country—whether Hutu, Tutsi, or Twa—identifies with a clan.

Historically, Rwandan women held traditional roles: rearing

STEALING A BRIDE

A man kidnapping a woman to make her his wife is an old custom in Rwanda. Although human rights groups protest strongly, the practice of bride stealing (also called marriage by abduction or forced marriage) still occurs in many rural areas.

In some cases of bride stealing, a man with a weapon will enter a household and simply force a girl or young woman to go with him. In other cases, he follows her and stops her when she is walking alone. He brings her to his house, where he rapes her and keeps her for several days. If she can't escape, everyone in the village considers her to be the man's new wife. The man then holds a ceremony, at which he formally asks the girl's parents to forgive him for his act. He may offer to exchange a cow, other goods, or money for his stolen bride.

Government officials have criticized this practice and have passed a law that punishes it with twenty years in prison. However, they rarely enforce the law, as many Rwandans see it as a tradition that should be protected.

children, maintaining the home, and keeping household gardens. After the genocide of 1994, however, women began to play a more active role in Rwandan politics. The country's new constitution guarantees that women will hold at least 30 percent of the seats in the legislature.

Genocide left Rwanda with a large population of widows and orphans, who struggled to make ends meet. Some joined farming cooperatives, where members grow cash crops such as coffee and gather other valuable items such as honey, wild mushrooms, and medicinal herbs. Cooperatives also benefit the Twa, who can no longer gather food or hunt on their traditional lands.

Hutu and Tutsi usually marry within their own umuryango and ubwoko, but intermarriage between members of different groups sometimes occurs. According to tradition, elder members of two families arrange marriages among their younger members. The groom's family customarily gives a gift to the bride's family. This gift, called the bride-price, is still an important part of marriage negotiation in modern Rwanda. The groom's family members see the task of raising the bride-price as a way to help the family attain higher status.

A woman holds her child in a remote Rwandan village. Even the most isolated areas of the country have seen population growth.

Members of a Twa clan greet visitors to their village. Almost one third of Rwanda's Twa people died in the 1994 genocide. Many of the survivors struggle against poverty and disease as well as discrimination.

Twa marriages take place when a groom announces his engagement to a bride, who brings a small dowry of food or goods to her new in-laws. Sometimes, a young girl simply moves into her fiancé's home. The man announces the marriage and then offers a gift of food or goods for taking the girl away from her family. Some Twa husbands take several wives, if they can support more than one.

Rwandan family and social structure has begun to change in recent years. For example, the pressure of limited land for an ever-growing population is making a social group called the *umuhana* more important. An umuhana is a community that includes several families who share land, labor, and other resources. In addition, the tradition of arranged marriages and bride-price payment are slowly dying out, especially in the towns and cities.

Visit www.vgsbooks.com for links to websites with additional information about daily life in Rwanda. Read about the latest efforts to preserve tradition while encouraging respect for individuals, especially between men and women and between different clans.

CHILD-FRIENDLY SCHOOLS

The 1994 genocide orphaned more than eight hundred thousand Rwandan children. Some have no surviving family members at all. Many children became refugees, and others got hurt or disabled in the fighting. To answer their special needs, Rwanda has established "child-friendly schools," which both teach and shelter young genocide victims.

The first of these, Rubingo School, serves 1,200 students near Kigali. The school educates the students and also makes sure they are well fed, healthy, and living in safe places. The Rwandan government hopes to apply this "child-friendly" model to selected schools throughout the country.

Children share a desk in an elementary classroom in Kigali. Schools closed in the aftermath of the 1994 genocide, and many students never returned because their parents were afraid of further violence.

⊙ Education

The foundation of Rwanda's modern education system lies in colonial times, when Christian missionaries from Europe and the United States built local schools. Some farming families in colonial Rwanda sent their children to a few years of mission school before marriage. The Belgian administration also established schools to train civil servants (government workers) and engineers. Opportunities for higher education, however, were limited. While public schools operated in the cities, rural areas—where most of the people lived—lacked even elementary public schools.

Public education improved in the early twenty-first century, when the Rwandan government started a crash school-building program. It raised hundreds of primary and secondary schools throughout the country. By 2007 most Rwandan children—rural and urban—had access to local public schools. The government spends about 15 percent of its budget on education.

By law Rwandans must attend six years of elementary school, starting at the age of seven. Instruction begins in Kinyarwanda (Rwanda's official language) and then continues in English and French after grade four. Students may attend three years of a lower secondary school—commonly beginning at the age of fourteen. About 90 percent of elementary-age Rwandan children attend school, but only about 12 percent of eligible children attend secondary school. Those who have graduated from elementary school may pursue technical and vocational training.

Rwandans have limited choices for higher education. The National University of Rwanda opened its doors in 1963. It has a main campus in Butare and another in Ruhengeri. Kigali is home to the Kigali Institute of Science, Technology, and Management.

About 69 percent of Rwandan youth can read and write. About 59 percent of Rwandan adults can read and write.

Health

Rwanda's people face many serious health problems. Some of these problems are common throughout Africa, while others arise from Rwanda's recent history. Like many nations in East Africa, Rwanda lacks enough trained doctors and nurses, local health clinics, and hospitals. Children often do not get vaccinations (shots) against serious diseases such as measles, diphtheria, and tetanus. People in remote areas have no medical facilities, and cities face a shortage of medicines.

A mother puts her baby into the sling of a weight scale at a small health center in Burera. Child health services struggle to provide care to as many families as possible despite medicine and staff shortages.

The civil war of the early 1990s and the genocide of 1994 caused a Rwandan refugee crisis. More than two million people fled the country. Refugee camps in the DRC, Uganda, and Tanzania sheltered them. Contagious diseases such as typhoid ran rampant through the camps. Many people still inhabit these camps and suffer from a lack of food, clean water, and basic sanitation (trash and sewage removal).

Common diseases in Rwanda include dysentery, tuberculosis, malaria, and trypanosomiasis (sleeping sickness). Disease is common in areas with poor sanitation and water pollution. Only about 40 percent of Rwandans have access to safe drinking water. Many Rwandan families suffer from malnutrition. Rwanda's land does not provide enough food to support its dense and growing population. Children have inadequate protein in their diet, which causes health problems as they grow.

Rwanda also has a very high rate of infection with human immunodeficiency virus (HIV), which causes acquired immunodeficiency syndrome (AIDS). HIV spreads through sexual contact, contaminated blood, and the use of dirty needles. Rapes that occurred during the 1994 genocide, as well as forced marriages, have contributed to high rates of HIV infection. Health officials estimate that more than 10 percent of Rwanda's adult population has HIV. In Rwanda about fifty thousand people die every year of AIDS, leaving thousands of orphaned children.

This refugee camp in Amahoro National Stadium in Kigali housed more than twenty thousand people during and after the 1994 genocide.

A pharmacist at a Butera HIV treatment center holds a **sample of an AIDS drug.**

The AIDS epidemic in Rwanda has caused widespread suffering and death. But there are fewer than five hundred doctors in Rwanda, and hospitals have a shortage of equipment and trained staff. So Rwandans who have AIDS often search for help outside the medical system. Many of them visit herbalists, who practice in their homes and in small shops in Rwandan cities. Using remedies made from plants and ground minerals, herbalists promise to help cure AIDS symptoms, such as skin rashes. But their work has come under fire from the central government. Rwandan officials have arrested many herbalists and have shut down their small clinics for fraud. As long as the medical system remains understaffed and underfunded, however, herbalism will remain alive and well.

Rwanda's infant mortality rate (the number of Rwandan babies that die within a year of their birth) is eighty-six per one thousand births. This rate is one of the highest in East Africa. Life expectancy in Rwanda is low: forty-six years for males and forty-eight years for females. These statistics are slowly improving as Rwanda's general health conditions and political stability improve.

CULTURAL LIFE

A common culture unites all social classes in Rwanda. Regardless of their ethnic group or location, all Rwandans share the same language, literature, cuisine, and other cultural traditions. They take pride in Rwanda's long precolonial history as a complex, well-organized kingdom—one of the strongest in East Africa. Rwandans of the twenty-first century are looking to their historic cultural traditions to help them overcome the bitter divisions of their recent past.

Religion

Rwandans practice traditional religion, or animism, as well as faiths outsiders brought in. Animism is a worldview in which spirits inhabit natural places, beings, things, and the everyday world. Imana is Rwandan animism's supreme being, and *abazimu* are the spirits of ancestors. Rwandan families honor these spirits with sacrifices and rituals to prevent illness and bad luck. One familiar and powerful abazimu is Ryangombe. In northern Rwanda, animists

honor Nyabingi, a spirit similar to Ryangombe. Less than 1 percent of all Rwandans still practice only animist rituals. Many more animists also belong to monotheistic (one-god) religions such as Islam and Christianity.

The Christian faith arrived in Rwanda in the 1890s with the first Catholic and Protestant missionaries. Under the protection of the colonial government, Christian missionaries built schools to educate Rwandans and held church services to convert them. Many Hutu leaders attended Catholic seminaries, or schools, which helped to train Hutus to administer Rwanda after independence. About 56 percent of Rwandans are Catholic. Protestant groups claim about 37 percent.

Many Rwandans abandoned Christianity in the 1990s because of some Christian leaders' association with the Hutu government's human rights abuses. Islam has been growing stronger in Rwanda since the civil war and genocide. About 5 percent of Rwandans are

Muslims, or followers of Islam. Almost 2 percent of Rwandans do not belong to any religious group.

Language and Literature

All Rwandans speak Kinyarwanda, the country's official language. People in the eastern Democratic Republic of Congo and southern Uganda also speak it. Kinyarwanda belongs to the Bantu family of languages spoken throughout central and southern Africa. Kinyarwanda is similar to Kirundi, the language of Burundi. Rwandans and Burundians can easily understand one another.

Rwandans use Kinyarwanda in everyday conversation, in primary school, and in most shops and other businesses. Some Rwandans use Kiswahili (often called Swahili), a widely known Bantu language, when they do business with other African countries. Written Swahili and Kinyarwanda both use the Latin alphabet.

Belgians brought the French language to Rwanda in the early twentieth century. French remains the medium of instruction in some Rwandan secondary schools and universities. However, English has begun to rival French as the most important foreign language used in Rwanda. Most secondary schools and universities use English as their main language of instruction. Many Rwandan refugees returning from Kenya and Uganda—former British colonies—have become English speakers.

Rwanda's oral, or spoken, literature derives from two sources: the royal tradition and the popular tradition. The royal tradition includes four major sets of texts: the Ubucurabwenge (genealogies, or family histories), Ubwiru (rituals), Ibisigo (poetry), and Ibitekerezo (myths about former kings). The popular tradition includes many types of folk literature, such as family histories; poetry about heroes, hunting, and the farming life; proverbs and other sayings; and riddles. It also includes the lyrics to many kinds of songs, such as praise, love, lullaby, work, and army songs. Modern Rwandans still enjoy folk literature and songs performed by professional storytellers at festivals, weddings, and public ceremonies.

Most modern Rwandan writers have worked in French. Alexis

SPEAKING KINYARWANDA

Learn a few simple phrases in Rwanda's native language.

Amakuru (ah-mah-koo-roo):
 how are you
Imbabazi (eem-ba-ba-zee):
 excuse me
Muraho (moora-hoh): hello
Murakoze (moora-kohzay):
 thank you
Oya (oh-yah): no
Yego (yay-goh): yes

Kagame was a scholar of Rwandan literature, history, and language who also wrote tales and poetry of his own. One of Rwanda's best-known novels is J. Saverio Naigiziki's *L'Optimiste* (the Optimist). It relates the story of a marriage between a Hutu husband and Tutsi wife. Naigiziki also describes traditional village life in *Escapade Ruandaise* (Rwandan Adventure).

The 1994 genocide is the subject matter for many Rwandans. Yolande Mukagasana explains her experiences during the genocide in *La mort ne veut pas de moi* (Death Doesn't Want Me) and *N'aie pas peur de savoir* (Don't Be Afraid to Know). Tutsi poet Jean-Baptiste Mutabaruka laments the massacre in his poem *Les chants du tom-tom* (Songs of the Drum). Benjamin Sehene wrote two books about these events, including *Le piège ethnique* (The Ethnic Trap) and *Le feu sous la soutane* (Fire Under the Cassock).

Music and Dance

Rwanda has many traditional musical instruments. The *lulunga* is a harplike instrument with eight strings. It accompanies singing and dancing. The smaller *kalimba* is a handheld wooden instrument with narrow metal keys plucked by the thumbs.

As in much of African music, drums play a key role in Rwandan music. Drumming is the most important form of music played in public. Drum orchestras contain drums of different pitches. With drum accompaniment, professional singers and dancers perform at weddings, to celebrate births, at harvesttime, and for funerals.

A drummer displays a **traditional drum** made of wood and animal skin. He plays it to accompany dancers.

An **Intore dancer** flings back his animal hair headdress with the force of his movements. This dance celebrates the bravery of a clan's warriors.

The *ikinimba* is a dance that presents the stories of Rwanda's heroes and kings. The Intore Dance Troupe is a group that originated in the court of the mwami.

Modern popular music in Rwanda borrows from Afrobeat and Highlife, western African styles that have spread throughout the continent. One of the most popular musicians is the guitarist Aime Murefu, who plays a local version of rock and the blues. The group Ingeli, led by Jean Paul Samputu, sings and plays traditional, modern, and gospel music.

Crafts

A lively tradition of handicrafts thrives in Rwanda. The country is known for beautiful mats and baskets woven from reeds, banana stalks, leaves, and papyrus fiber. In Rwanda owning fine baskets is a sign of prosperity and high status.

Weavers dye some of the reeds white, black, or red and use them to make complex geometric designs. They also decorate some of their work with beads and stones. Rwandans often use woven mats as room dividers. And because metal goods are scarce, woven baskets make useful food containers. Weavers assemble durable containers from thick coils of woven reeds.

Wood-carvers make bowls, jugs, utensils, drums, and pipes. Carved wood also goes into other musical instruments as well as handcrafted toys, furniture, and canoes. The Twa people have a long tradition of pottery making. They create bowls, jugs, pots, vases, and many other useful and decorative household items from fired clay. A group of painters in the eastern Rwandan town of Nyakarimbi are famous for using cow dung in their works. These and other works are on display at the National Museum of Rwanda in Butare.

Sports and Recreation

Soccer is Rwanda's most popular sport—both informally and formally. Children and adults play in the streets and open spaces in towns and villages. Kigali's Amahoro National Stadium hosts regular season matches as well as the national championship and international matches. On game days, millions of Rwandans tune in for soccer broadcasts on radio and television.

The country's professional soccer league boasts some of the best players in Africa. Rayon Sports, one of the leading teams, vies every year for the Rwandan title. But Armée Patriotique Rwandaise (APR), a powerhouse team formed by the Rwandan Patriotic Front after the civil war, usually wins. The top players in the country play for APR.

Rwanda's national soccer team, nicknamed the Wasps, wears blue, green, and yellow. The Wasps have twice won the Council of

A player from the Cameroon national soccer team, the Indomitable Lions, tackles a player for Rwanda's Wasps team *(right)* during the 2006 African Cup of Nations.

Several well-known films are set in Rwanda. *Gorillas in the Mist* (1988) describes the life and death of famous gorilla researcher Dian Fossey. The genocide of 1994 inspired *Hotel Rwanda* (2004), *Shake Hands with the Devil: The Journey of Roméo Dallaire* (2004), *Shooting Dogs* (2005), *Sometimes in April* (2005), and *Back Home* (2006).

East and Central Africa Football Associations (CECAFA) Cup. (Soccer is called football in most places outside the United States.) The Wasps qualified for their first African Cup of Nations championship in 2004. Some skilled Rwandan players moved to professional teams in Europe. For example, Olivier Karekezi played in Sweden, where he was a leading goal scorer. Désiré Mbonabucya played for K. Sint-Truidense V. V., a Belgian club.

Some city dwellers in Rwanda enjoy tennis and golf. The Kigali Golf Club, built in the 1980s, lies along the road between the capital and the airport. It is Rwanda's only eighteen-hole course. This club hosts a national amateur championship every year.

Outdoor sports, such as white-water rafting, sailing, and cross-country running, are gaining popularity. Rwandans also enjoy chess, checkers, and a board game called *mancala,* which is popular throughout Africa. Mancala players move stones or dried beans around a rectangular board with two rows of six cups. The object is to capture all of the opponent's pieces. The game demands careful strategy and good math skills.

Visit www.vgsbooks.com for links to websites with additional information about Rwandan cultural life. Practice phrases in Kinyarwanda, listen to samples of Rwandan traditional music, and play an online version of the game mancala.

⊙ Holidays and Festivals

Rwandan Christians observe Christianity's traditional holidays, including Easter and Christmas. Rwandan Muslims celebrate Ramadan, a month of prayer and fasting, among other holy days. Animists in Rwanda honor various spirits with celebrations that feature music, dancing, and dramatic costumes and masks. For example, every July members of the religious society called *babandwa* honor the spirit Ryangombe.

Muslim men converse outside the al-Fatah mosque in Kigali.

Rwanda has a busy calendar of national celebrations. January 28 is Democracy Day. On April 7, Genocide Memorial Day, Rwandans commemorate the terrible events of 1994. May 1 is Labor Day, when workers take a rest. July 1, Independence Day, marks the end of Rwanda's history as a Belgian colony. This holiday quickly gives way to Liberation Day on July 4, when Rwandans celebrate the RPF's 1994 liberation of Kigali, which ended both genocide and dictatorship in Rwanda. Rwandans celebrate the harvest festival Umuganura in August. At that time, they dedicate the first fruits of the fields to Imana and feast late into the night. On September 25, Rwandans celebrate Kamarampaka Day. (*Kamarampaka* means "referendum" in Kinyarwanda.) This holiday marks the day in 1961 when popular vote ended Rwanda's monarchy. October 26 is Armed Forces Day.

Food

The most common foods in the Rwandan diet are sweet potatoes, plantains, cassavas (also called manioc), millet, beans, and corn. Plantains are less-sweet relatives of bananas. Cooks prepare them by frying, boiling, grilling, or stewing. Rwandans eat the starchy roots of the cassava plant alone or with grilled meat. They may make cassavas into flour, or they may boil and then fry them. Pounded cassava root is the main ingredient in *foufou*, a dumpling-like dish popular throughout sub-Saharan Africa (the part of Africa south of the Sahara).

Beef is rare in much of Rwanda, mainly because cattle represent a valuable form of household property. People rarely kill cattle for meat.

Tutsis from Rwanda and Uganda meet at the Rwandan border to trade cattle. Cattle ownership is still an important status symbol in rural areas.

Some Rwandans raise chickens and goats to eat. Hunting for warthogs, antelopes, and crocodiles provides game meat for people living in remote areas.

Many rural Rwandans start their day with a breakfast of sweet potatoes baked in an open fire. A stew of millet, sorghum, and corn accompanies the potatoes. City dwellers may eat bread with coffee or tea early in the morning.

Meals taken at midday and in the evening are usually heavier than breakfast. *Umutsima* is a dish made with cassava and corn. *Isombe* combines cassava leaves, eggplant, and spinach. Tilapia is a freshwater fish that finds its way into many different stews, soups, and other dishes. Rwandans make peanut stew from chicken, ginger, okra, spices, and mashed peanuts. They also enjoy *mizuzu*, a tasty dish of peeled and fried plantains.

Snacks of fruit and bread are common during the day. The most common fruits in Rwanda are bananas, mangoes, papayas, and avocados. Vendors in villages and city markets offer roasted peanuts and corn. Rwandans enjoy beer, and many of them brew alcoholic drinks at home using fermented sorghum or corn.

PLANTAIN CHEESE BAKE

This semisweet menu item is served as a side dish in Rwanda. If you add an additional ¼ cup sugar, you could serve it as a cheesy dessert. (Fresh fruit usually serves as a cooling dessert in tropical Africa.)

4 tbsp. olive oil

2 ripe plantains, peeled and sliced into thin rounds

1 cup low-fat cottage cheese

1 tsp. cinnamon

1 tsp. sugar

3 egg yolks

3 egg whites

butter or vegetable oil for oiling a pan

½ cup dry bread crumbs

1. Preheat oven to 350°F. Heat oil until very hot in large frying pan. Carefully fry plantain rounds in oil until brown on both sides. Remove plantain rounds from pan and drain on paper towels.
2. Mix cheese, cinnamon, and sugar in a bowl.
3. Beat egg yolks with a fork in another bowl. Beat egg whites with an electric beater until stiff, in a third bowl. Gently fold egg whites into yolks.
4. Grease a loaf pan well with butter or oil. Sprinkle the bottom with bread crumbs.
5. Spread one-quarter of the egg mixture in the loaf pan. Add a layer of one-quarter of the fried plantains. Cover with a quarter of the cheese mixture. Repeat to make four layers.
6. Bake in oven at 350°F for 40 minutes.

Serves 4.

THE ECONOMY

The civil war and genocide of the early 1990s devastated Rwanda's economy. Many farmers died in the fighting or fled the country. Rioting in Kigali destroyed shops, small factories, and entire neighborhoods. The strife temporarily halted Rwanda's trade with foreign nations. In 1994 its gross domestic product (GDP)—the total value of goods and services produced in the country in a year—fell 50 percent.

Rwanda's GDP began to rise again in 1995, when the economy grew more than 9 percent. Foreign countries and the United Nations provided aid programs and grants to help Rwanda rebuild. It remains one of the poorest countries in the world, however, with an annual income of about $1,300 per person.

As an agricultural nation, Rwanda is vulnerable to poor weather. In 2003 East Africa experienced a severe drought. Low rainfall in Rwanda affected the harvests of both food staples and export crops. In 2004 growing conditions improved, while manufacturing and service busi-

nesses expanded with help from rising foreign investment. Economic growth continues at the rate of about 3 percent per year.

In 2007 Rwanda still depended on foreign aid for about half its national budget. But after ten years of political stability, it has attracted some foreign investment. In addition, the government has privatized (sold to private owners) some state-owned businesses. This helps the government save on their operating costs. The new private companies also attract outside investment and pay some of their income back to the public treasury in taxes.

◯ Agriculture

Rwanda is largely a nation of subsistence farmers—farmers who grow just enough to feed their families, with little or no extra crops to sell. Most people live in small communities. They grow food for their families and for sale at local markets. Rwandan families typically own several small plots of land. Some of the plots are far from

A woman pours samples at a **coffee-tasting event in Maraba.** Specialty coffee has become an important export for Rwanda.

home. This practice ensures a steady supply of food in case of drought in one area.

About 88 percent of the labor force works in the agricultural sector, which contributes 39 percent of Rwanda's GDP. Its most important food crops are plantains, sweet potatoes, sorghum, beans, and cassava. In irrigated fields, farmers can raise rice and taro, another nutritious plant. Rwanda's most important cash crop is coffee. It also has tobacco, flower, and tea plantations (large farms).

For centuries cattle have been Rwandans' key store of wealth. Families raise cattle for their milk and pasture them near their homes. They trade cattle for land and sometimes offer cattle in marriage negotiations. For these reasons, Rwandans generally do not raise cattle for meat. Chickens, goats, and sheep are more important livestock for meat production.

Rwanda's coffee growers got a big boost in 2006, when Starbucks began buying their beans. The international coffee roaster and retailer packages Rwandan coffee as Rwanda Blue Bourbon. The name comes from the blue green color of unroasted Rwandan coffee beans. This deal is helping many farmers recover from the 1990s, when civil war and genocide nearly ended Rwandan coffee growing altogether.

Traditionally, farm fields stayed in the possession of a local clan. Families could not sell or give land to outsiders. But Rwanda's rapidly growing population faces a serious land shortage. To help solve this problem, the government has passed several land reform measures. These allow private buyers to purchase and improve farmland. More productive seed strains, new irrigation projects, and better use of fertilizer may also help Rwanda make the most of its limited land.

Several agricultural programs are helping Rwanda become self-sufficient in food production (meet its own basic food needs). For example, the New Rice for Africa (NERICA) project crosses strains of African and Asian rice. This creates a plant that is hardier and more pest-resistant. Its better crop yields keep rice prices low and help poor families in Rwanda avoid malnutrition.

Services

The service sector in Rwanda has been growing rapidly since the mid-1990s. Service businesses—including banks, insurance companies, real estate firms, retail stores, tour operators, hotels, restaurants, and transportation and communication companies—now make up about 37 percent of Rwanda's GDP and employ about 9 percent of the labor force.

This is the fastest-growing sector in the country's economy. As more people move into the cities, demand for services rises. Service businesses also attract outside investment. Foreign companies establish local branches and hire Rwandans as managers and staff.

Visit www.vgsbooks.com for links to websites with additional facts and statistics about Rwanda's economy. Learn about the country's major imports and exports and listen to radio broadcasts from Radio Rwanda.

Manufacturing and Industry

Before the events of the 1990s, Rwanda's manufacturing sector was small and poorly developed. Most manufacturing occurred in Kigali, where heavy fighting occurred. The civil war paralyzed manufacturing. It damaged factories, drove off workers, and closed businesses. Many urban residents, including managers and skilled workers, fled the country.

The sector took ten years to revive. By 2004 manufacturing was providing about 22 percent of Rwanda's GDP and employing about 3 percent of its labor force. Its largest industry is food processing (preparing and packaging grains, vegetables, and rice). Brewers and bottlers produce juice, soft drinks, milk, beer, and bottled water for market. Cement plants have grown rapidly as Rwanda has rebuilt homes and infrastructure (public works such as bridges). The country also has a small textile (clothing) industry, as well as factories that make plastic and household consumer goods.

Rwanda is promoting manufacturing investment by outsiders. It is trying to attract businesses that will prepare goods, such as clothing and food, for export. The country is also trying to develop new industry, such as machinery and electrical equipment manufacturing.

Mining and Energy

Mining provides about 1 percent of Rwanda's GDP. Its most important mineral resource is cassiterite. Other Rwandan mining operations extract wolframite, columbite-tantalite (coltan), gold, and gemstones (including diamonds and sapphires).

Mining of gold, gemstones, and other valuable resources has drawn Rwanda into conflict with the Democratic Republic of Congo. With war and weak civil authority in eastern DRC, Rwandan and Ugandan forces have moved into the region and battled over mines and resources. Rwandan companies have illegally mined valuable minerals there, brought them into Rwanda, and then exported them.

Rwanda has very limited energy resources. It must import all of its oil and most of its natural gas. It has small hydroelectric projects on its rivers. For example, Rwanda operates the Ruzizi Dam with Burundi and the DRC. Electrical power is in short supply, and Rwanda's cities experience frequent power outages.

Lake Kivu holds a large underwater reserve of methane gas. Rwanda has made an agreement

COLTAN CONFLICT

Coltan mining is an increasingly important industry in Africa. Refineries turn this mineral into a metal powder called tantalum, which is worth about one hundred dollars per pound (0.45 kilogram) on the open market.

Coltan mining is a key part of Rwanda's mining industry. But it has also sparked violent conflict in eastern DRC. Rebel groups, which include many exiled Rwandans, control much of the land in this region. These groups take over mines by force, refine tantalum, and sell it abroad. They use the money to buy arms. In this way, the coltan market—and the world's growing demand for electronics—is feeding DRC's long-standing civil conflict.

with foreign companies to draw on this resource. Pumps will bring the gas-saturated water to the surface, where machines can draw off the methane to generate electricity. If successful, this project will allow Rwanda to meet all its own energy needs as well as power new industries and export energy to its neighbors.

Trade

Since the late 1990s, Rwanda has run a trade deficit. This means the country imports (buys) more from other countries than it exports (sells) to them.

Rwanda imports machinery, fuel, chemicals, and consumer goods. Its most important sources of imported goods are Kenya, Uganda, Tanzania, and the United Arab Emirates.

Rwanda's most important export is coffee, which provides more than a quarter of its export earnings. However, this vital cash crop is subject to swings in the world market price. In recent years, the falling price of coffee has reduced export income for Rwanda and other coffee-producing African countries.

Rwanda's other important agricultural exports are tea and pyrethrum, a flower used in pesticides. Rwanda also exports quinquina, a tree bark processed for use in beverages.

A NATURAL PESTICIDE

The bug-busting properties of pyrethrum flowers, which grow in Rwanda, came to light several hundred years ago. According to one account, some soldiers were resting in a large field of these chrysanthemum plants. When they awoke, lice and other insects that had been bothering them were all dead. Pyrethrum is nontoxic to humans and is an ingredient in many different insecticides. But since it breaks down in sunlight, it is not effective on crops.

Pyrethrum chrysanthemum fields surround a village near Ruhengeri.

Workers make **rope from the fibers of the sisal plant.** Much of the rope will be woven into baskets for export.

Rwanda's mineral exports include titanium, molybdenum, and columbite-tantalite (coltan), a mineral that is refined into tantalum. Tantalum's primary use is in electronic equipment, such as cell phones and DVD players. In years when its price is high, coltan contributes more to Rwanda's trade balance than any other export.

Rwanda exports its goods to Kenya, Tanzania, Indonesia, Germany, China, and the United Kingdom. The country has joined the Free Trade Area of the Common Market for Eastern and Southern Africa (COMESA). Rwanda has also joined the East African Community (EAC), a group of nations that, among other goals, pledges to reduce tariffs (taxes) on products traded among them.

Communications and Media

Rwanda has limited telephone service. Landlines serve Kigali and a few of the larger towns, but most people rely on cell phones. Rwandans have ten times as many cell phones as landline telephones. Relay towers in Kigali and the provincial capitals provide access to the network.

Rwanda has two publicly owned television networks. But electric service is rare outside the cities, and very few people have televisions. Most Rwandans get information and entertainment via transistor radio. The country has eight FM radio stations. Foreign stations, including Voice of America (VOA) and British Broadcasting Corporation (BBC), also broadcast to Rwanda.

Two **radio journalists** broadcast the first program of a new Rwandan station, Radio 10, in 2004. The station broadcasts in both French and English.

About two thousand Rwandan individuals and businesses have direct access to the Internet through a single Internet service provider (ISP) in Kigali. Most Rwandans use small Internet cafés, which offer access at hourly rates. The number of websites outside the country dealing with Rwandan culture, history, and current affairs is growing. Rwandan exiles in the United States, Africa, and Europe run many of these sites.

Transportation and Tourism

The road network in Rwanda links its capital, Kigali, with smaller towns in the other provinces. On the main roads, trucks and vans jostle, and pedestrians often crowd the margins. In the cities, traffic is usually a chaotic gridlock of walkers, vendors, bicyclists, trucks, cars, motorcycles, and minivans.

The most common mode of long-distance transportation in Rwanda is the "share taxi." Share taxis are vans and minibuses that wait for passengers at fixed stops. When the vehicle fills, it sets off for a distant town or for the border. It drops

In the early twenty-first century, surveyors began laying out Rwanda's first-ever potential rail route, which would connect Kigali with Burundi to the south and Tanzania to the east. The railway would allow Rwanda to export its goods more easily via the Indian Ocean port of Dar es Salaam, Tanzania.

passengers wherever they need to go. Within the cities, "taxi-motors" (converted motorcycles) carry paying passengers.

The Kigali International Airport has the largest airfield in the country. Rwanda has air links to Nairobi, Kenya; Bujumbura, Burundi; and Dar es Salaam, Tanzania. Long-distance buses also link Rwanda with neighboring countries.

In the early twenty-first century, while recovering from its civil war, Rwanda began to attract tourists. Visitors explore the Virunga Mountains and join expeditions to see mountain gorillas. Studying the Nyungwe Forest is a popular activity for ecotourists, who travel to learn about and help preserve nature. Lake Kivu is a popular destination for boating and other water sports. Kigali attracts outsiders with its bustling markets and lively streets. Many sites connected with the 1994 genocide help tourists learn lessons from a dark period in Rwandan history.

◎ The Future

Rwanda has largely recovered from the tragic events of the 1990s. The economy is growing steadily, and ethnic violence is waning. The country has held peaceful elections, and its troublesome militias have disbanded. Rwanda still needs foreign investment, though. It cannot

A mountain gorilla eats leaves in Volcanoes National Park. The gorillas attract ecotourists interested in saving endangered species.

develop complex new industries, mines, and energy sources without outside help.

Rwanda's goal of creating a mixed economy, in which industry and services contribute as much as agriculture, is a difficult one. Most Rwandans are farmers. Their lives are closely tied to their rural villages and deeply rooted in their fields. But eventually the dwindling amount of available land will force many Rwandans to move to the cities. This may fuel urban problems as well as social conflict.

One promising industry for the future is tourism. Rwanda offers many interesting sights and activities for visitors. Tourism allows Rwanda to earn money without depleting its natural resources or polluting its environment. Rwanda can then invest its tourism income in new construction and new businesses.

Rwanda is also finally benefiting from the world's attention. The international community's failure to stop the 1994 genocide caused a public outcry in the United States, in Western Europe, and in the member nations of the UN. All developed an interest in a stable, peaceful Rwanda. The wealthier nations in this group are making investments, sending food and medical help, and trying to prevent further conflict. As a result, Rwanda's future prospects are much brighter than its recent past.

5000 B.C.   Northern Africa's vast savanna transforms into the Sahara, driving hunter-gatherers and settled farmers southward in search of game and well-watered land.

A.D. 1000   Farmers and cattle herders settle eastern Africa's region of highlands and lakes.

1600s   Hutu, Tutsi, and Twa peoples present in Rwanda.

1700s   The Tutsi Abanyiginya clan emerges as a royal dynasty.

1802   Mutara II Rwogera becomes the mwami and rules until 1853.

1860   Mwami Kigeri Rwabugiri comes to the throne. Under his leadership, the Tutsi emerge as the upper class of Rwandan society.

1863   Rwabugiri assembles large armies to defend Rwanda from outsiders.

1885   Germany claims Rwanda as part of its colony German East Africa.

1894   Gustav Adolf von Goetzen, a German explorer, becomes the first European to visit Rwanda.

1914   World War I breaks out in Europe, with Germany fighting Belgium and Great Britain.

1916   Belgium invades Rwanda and seizes it from Germany.

1919   At the Paris Peace Conference, the Allies officially recognize Belgian control of Ruanda-Urundi.

1924   The League of Nations grants Belgium a mandate to rule Ruanda-Urundi.

1925   Ruanda-Urundi becomes a province of the colony of the Belgian Congo (which later becomes Zaire and then the Democratic Republic of the Congo (DRC).

1931   Charles Mutara III Rudahigwa becomes mwami and converts to Catholicism.

1933   The Belgian colony issues all Rwandans identity cards, which mark them as Tutsi, Hutu, or Twa.

1939   World War II breaks out in Europe.

1943   The government establishes new elected councils to advise the mwami in various matters.

1946   The United Nations confirms Belgian control of Rwanda after World War II.

1952   Belgian authorities set up a system of elected local councils, which remain largely under the control of Tutsi chiefs and subchiefs.

1957   Hutu leaders publish a declaration called the Hutu
        Manifesto, calling for more political and economic rights for
        the Hutu majority.

1959   The assassination of Mutara III sparks political conflict and violence.

1960   Hutu politicians win sweeping victories in legislative elections. Grégoire
        Kayibanda establishes a provisional government in preparation for inde-
        pendence.

1961   Dominique Mbonyumutwa overthrows the Tutsi monarchy and establishes a new
        government dominated by Hutus. Mbonyumutwa serves as the head of state and
        president.

1962   On July 1, Rwanda wins full independence. Grégoire Kayibanda becomes the presi-
        dent. The southern portion of Ruanda-Urundi becomes the separate nation of
        Burundi.

1963   Tutsi militias invade from Burundi and come within a few miles of Kigali before being
        defeated. The invasion sets off a massacre of several thousand Tutsis by the Hutu
        majority.

1973   Juvénal Habyarimana becomes the new leader of Rwanda, abolishing all political
        parties.

1986   Tutsi leader Paul Kagame forms the Rwandan Patriotic Front (RPF) in Uganda.

1990   The RPF invades Rwanda from the north. Civil war ensues.

1993   The government of Rwanda and the RPF sign a peace agreement in Arusha, Tanzania.

1994   In April President Habyarimana dies when his private jet is shot down. This event begins
        the Rwandan genocide. The genocide ends in July, when the RPF seizes Kigali.

1996   Several nations participate in the First Congo War, with Rwandan troops fighting in
        eastern DRC.

2000   The Rwandan legislature elects Paul Kagame as the new president.

2001   The government sets up a system of Gacaca courts to try those accused of order-
        ing the Rwandan genocide.

2003   Rwanda holds its first post-genocide presidential and legislative elections.

2007   The government abolishes the death penalty. Kagame pardons his imprisoned
        political rival, Pasteur Bizimungu.

Fast Facts

COUNTRY NAME Republic of Rwanda

AREA 10,169 square miles (26,338 sq. km)

MAIN LANDFORMS Albertine Rift Valley, Virunga Mountains, Congo-Nile Divide, Central Plateau, Eastern Savanna

HIGHEST POINT Mount Karisimbi, 14,787 feet (4,507 m) above sea level

LOWEST POINT Ruzizi River, 3,117 feet (950 m) above sea level

MAJOR RIVERS Akanyaru River, Kagera River, Kagitumba River, Mwogo River, Nyabarango River, Ruzizi River

ANIMALS antelopes, bushbucks, buffalo, chimpanzees, elands, elephants, gazelles, giraffes, hippopotamuses, hyenas, impalas, leopards, L'Hoest's monkeys, lions, mountain gorillas, olive baboons, Ruwenzori colobus monkey, vervet monkeys, warthogs, topis, zebras

CAPITAL CITY Kigali

OTHER MAJOR CITIES Gitarama, Butare, Ruhengeri, Cyangugu

OFFICIAL LANGUAGE Kinyarwanda

MONETARY UNIT Rwandan franc. 100 centimes = 1 Rwandan franc.

CURRENCY

Rwanda's currency is the Rwandan franc (RF). The currency comes in paper notes worth 5,000; 2,000; 1,000; 500; and 100 francs. The government reissued coins in 2003, for the first time in twenty years. Coins are worth 50, 20, 10, 5, 2, and 1 franc. The Rwandan franc originated in Belgium's colonial currency system. Rwandans also use the U.S. dollar in exchange for goods and services. Some individuals trade Rwandan francs for dollars on the black market. This illegal market lets outsiders trade dollars for francs at a much higher rate than the official rate used by Rwandan banks.

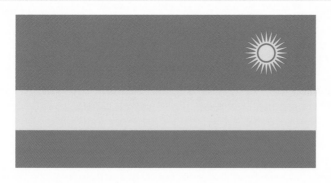

Rwanda adopted its flag on October 25, 2001. Alphonse Kirimobenecyo, an engineer and artist, designed the flag to symbolize unity, patriotism, and hope. Rwanda's former flag, dating from 1962, had become a symbol of ethnic divisions and genocide. It had vertical bands of red, yellow, and green with a large capital *R* in the central yellow band.

Rwanda's current flag has three horizontal bands. The top half of the flag is blue, with a yellow sun in the upper right corner. The blue stands for peace, and the sun with twenty-four rays stands for enlightenment and hope. Smaller yellow and green bands complete the lower half of the flag. The yellow stands for Rwanda's potential wealth, and the green stands for the country's natural resources.

Rwanda adopted its current national anthem, "Rwanda Nziza" (Rwanda, Our Beautiful Country) in 2002. Faustin Murigo wrote the lyrics, which celebrate Rwandan heroism, culture, and patriotism. Murigo wrote the words in Karubanda Prison. Captain Jean-Bosco Hashakaimana of the Rwandan army wrote the music. Below is an English translation of the first verse.

Rwanda, Our Beautiful Country
Rwanda, our beautiful and dear country,
Adorned with hills, lakes, and volcanoes,
Motherland, would be always filled of happiness,
Us all your children: Abanyarwanda
Let us sing your glory and proclaim your high facts.
You, maternal bosom of us all,
Would be admired forever, prosperous and covered with praises.

Visit www.vgsbooks.com for a link to a website where you can listen to Rwanda's national anthem, "Rwanda Nziza."

Flag National Anthem

DIAN FOSSEY (1932–1985) Dian Fossey was a scientist who made the study of Rwanda's mountain gorillas her life's work. She wrote *Gorillas in the Mist*, a famous book about her experiences. Born in San Francisco, California, she first visited Africa in 1963 and moved there in 1966 to work with paleontologist (scientist of prehistoric lifeforms) Louis Leakey. In 1967 she established Karisoke Research Center in the Virunga Mountains. She observed the gorillas every day and became acquainted with several, naming them and recording their lives. She sought to protect them from poachers and from disturbance by tourists. On December 26, 1985, she was murdered in her home. This crime remains unsolved.

GUSTAV ADOLF VON GOETZEN (1866–1910) Gustav Adolf von Goetzen was a German explorer known as the first European to set foot in Rwanda. Born in Scharfeneck, Germany, Goetzen trained as a lawyer, joined the German army, and was stationed in Rome. He first came to Africa in 1890 or 1891 on a hunting trip. In 1894 he led an expedition to claim and explore the inland region of Germany's new colony, German East Africa. He journeyed from the Indian Ocean coast of Tanzania across the Kagera River, through Rwanda to Lake Kivu, then onward to the Congo River and the Atlantic Ocean. Rwanda was one of the last regions of Africa to be explored by outsiders. Its high mountains, dense rain forests, and distance from the main trade routes made it difficult to reach. Goetzen later became a governor of German East Africa, which included the province of Ruanda-Urundi.

JUVÉNAL HABYARIMANA (1937–1994) Juvénal Habyarimana was president of Rwanda from 1973 to 1994, when his assassination touched off the Rwandan genocide. An ethnic Hutu, Habyarimana was born in Gisenyi Province. He seized power in 1973. He allowed no opposition parties and strictly limited all forms of political speech and activity. He helped promote ethnic strife between Hutus and Tutsis and supported the small Hutu militias that would play an important part in the genocide.

IMMACULÉE ILIBAGIZA (b. 1972) Immaculée Ilibagiza wrote *Left to Tell: Discovering God Amidst the Rwandan Holocaust* about her time in hiding during the Rwandan genocide. A Tutsi, Ilibagiza was born in Mataba and attended the National University of Rwanda. In 1994, while she was home for an Easter visit, her family home was attacked. She hid for three months with seven other women in the tiny bathroom of a Hutu neighbor's house. She lost her entire family in the genocide. Later, she moved to the United States. She works for the UN.

PAUL KAGAME (b. 1957) Paul Kagame was born in Gitarama. He was a founder of the Rwandan Patriotic Front (RPF), a Tutsi militia that supported more participation by the Tutsi minority in the Rwandan government. During the genocide of 1994, the RPF invaded Rwanda, defeating the Hutu forces in July, overthrowing the government, and ending the killing. Kagame became president of Rwanda in 2000.

GRÉGOIRE KAYIBANDA (1924–1976) Grégoire Kayibanda was a Hutu political leader who played a key role in Rwanda's drive for independence. He was born in Tare, in southern Rwanda. In 1959 he formed the Parmehutu party, a group that fought against Tutsi dominance as well as control of Rwanda by Belgium and the UN. After Rwanda gained independence in 1962, Kayibanda became the country's second president, following Dominique Mbonyumutwa. This marked the end of Rwanda's traditional Tutsi monarchy. In 1973 Kayibanda's defense minister, Juvénal Habyarimana, overthrew him.

CÉCILE KAYIREBWA (b. 1946) Cécile Kayirebwa is a musician, singer, and songwriter born in Kigali. She began her career with the Rwanda Song and Dance Circle when she was fifteen. In the 1980s, she moved to Belgium. There she learned French and began performing rhythm-and-blues and soul tunes. She studied at the Royal Museum for Central Africa in Belgium, and she joined Bula Sangoma, an African group in Belgium. Her first album was *Music from Rwanda*. She also performs with the group Arcadia.

ODETTE NYIRAMILIMO (b. 1956) Odette Nyiramilimo is a doctor and senator born in Kinunu. She served as the minister of social affairs from 2000 until 2003. She was expelled from school as a child because she is Tutsi, but she later attended medical school in Butare and became a doctor. With her husband, who is also a doctor, she founded a clinic in Kigali called Le Bon Samaritain (the Good Samaritan).

PAUL RUSESABAGINA (b. 1954) Paul Rusesabagina is a Hutu hotel manager who saved the lives of more than one thousand Tutsis and Hutus during the 1994 genocide. He was born in Murama, in Gitarama Province. Rusesabagina protected fleeing families in the rooms and on the grounds of the Hotel des Milles Collines in Kigali. The film *Hotel Rwanda* tells his story. He lives in Belgium.

JEAN PAUL SAMPUTU (b. 1962) Jean Paul Samputu is a singer and member of the Ingeli Dance Troupe of Rwanda. Born in Butare, he started his career with the group Nyampinga. In 1985 he recorded *Tegeka Isi*, his first solo album. Samputu sings in Kinyarwanda and three other African languages: Swahili, Lingala, and Luganda. He moved to Canada after losing his parents in the Rwandan genocide. In 2003 he won a Kora Award, the "African Grammy." His 2004 album *Testimony from Rwanda* was an international best seller. Samputu lives in the United States.

Conditions in Rwanda have stabilized, but the U.S. Department of State advises against travel to several of its neighboring countries. Before visiting Rwanda, check travel conditions at the Current Travel Warnings website (http://travel.state.gov/travel/cis_pa_tw/tw_1764.html).

AKAGERA NATIONAL PARK This park in eastern Rwanda is a good place for game-sighting safaris. Zebras, giraffes, elephants, water buffalo, crocodiles, hippos, and many antelope species roam the park.

BUTARE This city is the cultural capital of Rwanda, attracting students, artists, and performers of all kinds. Butare is home to the National University of Rwanda and the National Museum of Rwanda.

BYUMBA This town is the capital of Rwanda's Northern Province and is home to an SOS Children's Village. The village provides a home for children orphaned during the civil war and genocide.

HOTEL DES MILLES COLLINES This famous hotel in Kigali sheltered more than one thousand Tutsis and Hutus during the 1994 genocide. The film *Hotel Rwanda* (2004) features this hotel and its manager, Paul Rusesabagina.

KARISOKE RESEARCH CENTER This is the station on the slopes of Mount Karisimbi where U.S. scientist Dian Fossey carried out her research on Rwanda's endangered tribe of mountain gorillas. The station has not operated since the early 1990s, but tourists can still visit it.

KIGALI Rwanda's capital city is built on a series of hills and valleys. The city is home to lively markets, shaded boulevards, and the Kigali Memorial Centre, a genocide burial site, monument, and education center.

NTARAMA CHURCH An eerie memorial to the 1994 genocide, this church in rural Kigali City Province was the site of a brutal massacre of five thousand Tutsis who had fled there for refuge. The remains of many victims can be seen within the church, and several mass graves surround the building as a memorial to the dead.

NYUNGWE FOREST NATIONAL PARK Visitors to this park in southwestern Rwanda can track chimpanzees and twelve other primate species.

VOLCANOES NATIONAL PARK This park is home not only to volcanoes but also to a tribe of mountain gorillas. Visitors can observe the gorillas with a professional guide and view a gorilla graveyard, which is also the site of Dian Fossey's grave.

Abanyiginya: the Tutsi clan from which the mwami (kings) were selected

Aprosoma: a Hutu political party formed in 1957 by Joseph Gitera. The name is an acronym for the French name Association pour la Promotion Sociale de la Masse (Association for the Social Promotion of the Masses).

genocide: mass murder in order to destroy a specific racial, political, or cultural group

Interahamwe: small armed bands of Hutus who helped to carry out the 1994 genocide. The name means "those who work together."

International Criminal Tribunal for Rwanda (ICTR): a court set up to try those accused of coordinating the 1994 genocide

inzu: extended family, the basic unit of Rwandan society

Kinyarwanda: the official language of Rwanda, spoken by all Rwandans

mwami: the traditional king of Rwanda, selected from the Abanyiginya clan by a council of chiefs

Parmehutu: a Hutu political group formed by Grégoire Kayibanda in 1959 to promote Hutu participation in Rwanda's goverment. The name is an acronym for the French name Parti du Mouvement de l'Emancipation Hutu (Party of the Movement for Hutu Freedom).

rugo: a fenced compound consisting of houses, pastures, and gardens in which the Rwandan inzu, or extended family, makes its home

Rwanda National Union Party (UNAR): a Tutsi political party founded in 1959 that favored Rwanda's complete independence and the preservation of the Tutsi monarchy

Rwandan Patriotic Front (RPF): a Tutsi military group that invaded Rwanda in 1990, touching off a civil war. The RPF was also responsible for ending the 1994 genocide.

ubuhake: the traditional system of cattle ownership that once dominated Rwandan social and economic life

uburetwa: the traditional system of land use in Rwanda. It restricted Hutu workers to serving the Tutsi landowning aristocracy as laborers and tenants.

ubwoko: the largest Rwandan social group or clan. Rwanda has thirteen such clans.

United Nations Assistance Mission for Rwanda (UNAMIR): the small UN force sent to keep the peace in Rwanda in the early 1990s

Glossary

Selected Bibliography

Berkeley, Bill. *The Graves Are Not Yet Full: Race, Tribe, and Power in the Heart of Africa.* New York: Perseus Books, 2001.
A journalist describes his experiences in Rwanda during its civil war and genocide and in other troubled African nations such as Liberia. He believes that European colonization led to Africa's many tribal civil wars.

Chrétien, Jean-Pierre. *The Great Lakes of Africa: Two Thousand Years of History.* Cambridge, MA: Zone Books, 2006.
The author gives valuable information on the little-known precolonial history of the Great Lakes region, which includes Rwanda, Burundi, eastern DRC, western Tanzania, and Uganda. In particular, the book also analyzes the German and Belgian colonial governments in Rwanda.

Hatzfeld, Jean. *Machete Season: The Killers in Rwanda Speak.* New York: Picador, 2006.
The book records the experiences of ten friends, all from the same village, who took part in the Rwandan genocide.

Mushikiwabo, Louise, and Jack Kramer. *Rwanda Means the Universe: A Native's Memoir of Blood and Bloodlines.* New York: St. Martin's Press, 2006.
Mushikiwabo, a Tutsi living in the United States at the time of the genocide, describes what happened to members of her family. The authors also give a history of Rwanda's ethnic and social divisions.

Nyrop, Richard. *Rwanda: A Country Study.* Washington, DC: U.S. Government Printing Office, 1982.
This is a comprehensive handbook on Rwanda that gives background on the country's geography, climate, history, economy, society, political affairs, and culture.

Peterson, Scott. *Me against My Brother: At War in Somalia, Sudan, and Rwanda.* New York: Routledge, 2000.
The author reports on conflicts in Sudan, Somalia, and Rwanda. He gives vivid descriptions of terrible events and also provides some thoughts on how the genocide in Rwanda came about.

Population Reference Bureau. August 1, 2007.
http://www.prb.org (September 5, 2007)
The bureau offers current population figures, vital statistics, land area, and more. Special articles cover the latest environmental and health issues that concern each country, including Rwanda.

Prunier, Gérard. *The Rwanda Crisis: History of a Genocide.* New York: Columbia University Press, 1995.
This book provides a detailed and very interesting account of Rwanda's complex political situation leading up to the genocide of 1994.

Richburg, Keith B. *Out of America: A Black Man Confronts Africa.* **New York: Basic Books, 1997.**
The author is an African American journalist who spent several years in Rwanda and other East African nations. He compares his experiences to those of Africans he meets and finds his outlook on life much more American than African.

Rusesabagina, Paul, and Tom Zoellner. *An Ordinary Man: An Autobiography.* **New York: Viking, 2006.**
Rusesabagina was the manager of the Hotel des Milles Collines in Kigali, made famous by the 2004 film *Hotel Rwanda*. The authors describe his life and his experiences during the 1994 genocide, when he sheltered more than one thousand Tutsis and Hutus from murderous mobs.

Scherrer, Christian P. *Genocide and Crisis in Central Africa: Conflict Roots, Mass Violence, and Regional War.* **Westport, CT: Praeger, 2002.**
The author covers conflicts throughout the Great Lakes region of east central Africa. He traces the roots of the conflict to the events surrounding the independence of these nations after World War II.

Straus, Scott. *The Order of Genocide: Race, Power, and War in Rwanda.* **Ithaca, NY: Cornell University Press, 2006.**
The author interviews hundreds of people who took part in the 1994 genocide and examines the main causes for the tragedy. He faults the Rwandan government, the country's high population density, and traditional ethnic rivalry for creating a climate of fear and mistrust.

Taylor, Christopher C. *Sacrifice As Terror: The Rwandan Genocide of 1994.* **London: Berg, 1999.**
The author examines many aspects of Rwanda's Hutu-Tutsi rivalry to explain why the genocide took place.

The World Factbook. **August 16, 2007.**
https://www.cia.gov/library/publications/the-world-factbook/geos/rw.html (September 5, 2007).
This website features up-to-date information about the people, land, economy, and government of Rwanda. It also briefly covers transnational issues.

Berry, John A., and Carol Pott Berry. *Genocide in Rwanda: A Collective Memory.* **Washington, DC: Howard University Press, 1999.**
The editors interview soldiers, experts, and survivors about the 1994 genocide. The book includes texts of radio broadcasts that incited some Rwandans to commit mass murder.

Carr, Rosamond Halsey, and Ann Howard Halsey. *Land of a Thousand Hills: My Life in Rwanda.* **New York: Plume, 1999.**
This book is the memoir of Rosamond Halsey Carr, a New York fashion designer who moved to Rwanda and managed a flower plantation. She fled during the 1994 genocide but soon returned to Rwanda to rebuild her home.

Dallaire, Roméo. *Shake Hands with the Devil.* **New York: Carroll & Graf, 2004.**
A Canadian general who led the small UN force inside Rwanda during the 1994 genocide wrote this memoir. The author blames the UN and the United States for acting too slowly to prevent the tragedy.

Di Piazza, Francesca Davis. *Democratic Republic of Congo in Pictures.* **Minneapolis: Twenty-First Century Books, 2008.**
The Democratic Republic of Congo is Rwanda's neighbor to the west, and the two nations share both the problems of and solutions to ethnic conflict in the area. This book examines Congo's history, society, and culture, including its interactions with Rwanda.

Fossey, Dian. *Gorillas in the Mist.* **New York: Mariner Books, 2000.**
This popular book describes the author's work among Rwanda's mountain gorillas. She describes her long study of the gorillas and her attempts to protect them from poachers.

The Gorilla Organization
http://www.gorillas.org
This website is dedicated to Dian Fossey. It describes efforts to protect the quickly vanishing mountain gorillas, who are threatened by poachers and development.

Gourevitch, Philip. *We Wish to Inform You That Tomorrow We Will Be Killed with Our Families: Stories from Rwanda.* **New York: Picador, 1998.**
The author investigates the personal experiences of people in Rwanda during the genocide. His subjects include Paul Kagame and Paul Rusesabagina.

Ilibagiza, Immaculée, and Steve Erwin. *Left to Tell: Discovering God Amidst the Rwandan Genocide.* **Carlsbad, CA: Hay House, 2006.**
The author describes her terrifying experiences during the Rwandan genocide, when she hid from roving bands of killers for three months.

Jansen, Hanna. *Over a Thousand Hills I Walk With You.* **Minneapolis: Carolrhoda Books, 2006.**
Based on a true story, this novel follows the eight-year-old Jeanne through the days before and after the 1994 genocide. After losing her entire family in the massacre, Jeanne relies on her courage, wits, and good luck to survive.

Further Reading and Websites

January, Brendan. *Genocide.* **Minneapolis: Twenty-First Century Books, 2007.**
This book focuses on the genocides of the twentieth century, explaining what genocide is and discussing it in light of international law. It includes discussions of the Armenians, the Holocaust, the Cambodians of the killing fields, Tutsis of Rwanda, the Muslims of Bosnia, and non-Arabs in Darfur, Sudan.

Official Website of the Republic of Rwanda
http://www.gov.rw
This website gives general information about Rwanda, including basic facts, latest news, tourism information, and biographies of the president and the First Lady.

Rucyahana, John, and James Riordan. *The Bishop of Rwanda: Finding Forgiveness Amidst a Pile of Bones.* **Nashville: Thomas Nelson, 2007.**
A Tutsi bishop of the Anglican Church describes the effort to rebuild the church in Rwanda after the 1994 genocide.

vgsbooks.com
http://www.vgsbooks.com
Visit vgsbooks.com, the homepage of the Visual Geography Series®. You can get linked to all sorts of useful online information, including geographical, historical, demographic, cultural, and economic websites. The vgsbooks.com site is a great resource for late-breaking news and statistics.

Captions for photos appearing on cover and chapter openers:

Cover: A woman waits in the doorway of her house near Rusumo. The house has been decorated with cow-dung paintings traditional in the area.

pp. 4–5 Tea fields cover the mountainsides on the edge of Nyungwe Forest National Park.

pp. 8–9 Mount Sabinyo is the oldest of the volcanoes in Volcanoes National Park, which is home to endangered mountain gorillas and many other animals.

pp. 36–37 Buyers crowd around a woman selling bananas at the market in Nyakabuye, a town near Cyangugu in southwestern Rwanda.

pp. 46–47 Women and children perform a traditional dance, accompanied by drums and the clapping of spectators.

pp. 56–57 A man digs clay at a traditional brick factory. Lines of wet bricks, formed with wooden molds, dry along the edge of his trench.

Photo Acknowledgments

The images in this book are used with the permission of: © Ariadne Van Zandbergen, p. 4–5, 8–9, 11, 12, 15, 16, 21, 23, 36–37, 49, 50, 56–57, 64; © XNR Productions, pp. 6, 10; © Marli Miller/Visuals Unlimited, p. 14; © Louis Lesanges/The Bridgeman Art Gallery/Getty Images, p. 22; © National Anthropological Archives, Smithsonian Institution [NAA INV 06068301], p. 25; © AP Photo, p. 26; © Bettmann/CORBIS, p. 27; © Charlyn Zlotnik/Zuma Press, p. 28; © AP Photo/Jean-Marc Bouju, p. 29; © AP Photo/Ricardo Mazalan, p. 30; © Sean Sprague/The Image Works, p. 31; © Per-Andres Petterson/Getty Images, p. 33; © AP Photo/Rodrique Ngowi, p. 34; © Howard Sayer/Art Directors, pp. 38 (left), 42, 46–47; © Reinaldo Vargas/Art Directors, pp. 38 (right), 44, 54; © Roy Toft/National Geographic/Getty Images, p. 40; © Betty Press/Panos Pictures, p. 41; © Karl Blanchet/ZUMA Press, pp. 43, 45; © AP Photo/Riccardo Gangale, p. 51; © AP Photo/Karel Prinsloo, p. 53; © Jose Cendon/Stringer/Getty Images, p. 58; © Alison Jones/DanitaDelimont.com/ Alamy, p. 61; © Mike Goldwater/Alamy, p. 62; © Gianluigi Guercia/Stringer/ Getty Images, p. 63; © Audrius Tomonis—www.banknotes.com, p. 68.

Front cover: © Ariadne Van Zandbergen.